Praise fo

"Need-to-read inside information line—the best source in the business." – Daniel J. Moore, Member, Harris Beach LLP

"The *Inside the Minds* series is a valuable probe into the thoughts, perspectives, and techniques of accomplished professionals..." – Chuck Birenbaum, Partner, Thelen Reid & Priest

"Aspatore has tapped into a goldmine of knowledge and expertise ignored by other publishing houses." – Jack Barsky, Managing Director, Information Technology and CIO, ConEdison Solutions

"Unlike any other publisher—actual authors that are on the front lines of what is happening in industry." – Paul A. Sellers, Executive Director, National Sales, Fleet and Remarketing, Hyundai Motor America

"A snapshot of everything you need..." – Charles Koob, Co-Head of Litigation Department, Simpson Thacher & Bartlet

"Everything good books should be—honest, informative, inspiring, and incredibly well written." – Patti D. Hill, President, BlabberMouth PR

"Great information for both novices and experts." – Patrick Ennis, Partner, ARCH Venture Partners

"A rare peek behind the curtains and into the minds of the industry's best." – Brandon Baum, Partner, Cooley Godward

"Intensely personal, practical advice from seasoned deal-makers." – Mary Ann Jorgenson, Coordinator of Business Practice Area, Squire, Sanders & Dempsey

"Great practical advice and thoughtful insights." – Mark Gruhin, Partner, Schmeltzer, Aptaker & Shepard PC

"Reading about real-world strategies from real working people beats the typical business book hands down." – Andrew Ceccon, CMO, OnlineBenefits Inc.

"Books of this publisher are syntheses of actual experiences of real-life, hands-on, front-line leaders—no academic or theoretical nonsense here. Comprehensive, tightly organized, yet nonetheless motivational!" – Lac V. Tran, Senior Vice President, CIO, and Associate Dean, Rush University Medical Center

"Aspatore is unlike other publishers...books feature cutting-edge information provided by top executives working on the front lines of an industry." – Debra Reisenthel, President and CEO, Novasys Medical Inc.

www.Aspatore.com

Aspatore Books, a Thomson business, is the largest and most exclusive publisher of C-level executives (CEO, CFO, CTO, CMO, partner) from the world's most respected companies and law firms. Aspatore annually publishes a select group of C-level executives from the Global 1,000, top 250 law firms (partners and chairs), and other leading companies of all sizes. C-Level Business Intelligence™, as conceptualized and developed by Aspatore Books, provides professionals of all levels with proven business intelligence from industry insiders—direct and unfiltered insight from those who know it best—as opposed to third-party accounts offered by unknown authors and analysts. Aspatore Books is committed to publishing an innovative line of business and legal books, those which lay forth principles and offer insights that, when employed, can have a direct financial impact on the reader's business objectives, whatever they may be. In essence, Aspatore publishes critical tools—need-to-read as opposed to nice-to-read books—for all business professionals.

Inside the Minds

The critically acclaimed *Inside the Minds* series provides readers of all levels with proven business intelligence from C-level executives (CEO, CFO, CTO, CMO, partner) from the world's most respected companies. Each chapter is comparable to a white paper or essay and is a future-oriented look at where an industry/profession/topic is heading and the most important issues for future success. Each author has been carefully chosen through an exhaustive selection process by the *Inside the Minds* editorial board to write a chapter for this book. *Inside the Minds* was conceived in order to give readers actual insights into the leading minds of business executives worldwide. Because so few books or other publications are actually written by executives in industry, *Inside the Minds* presents an unprecedented look at various industries and professions never before available.

The Changing Role of Academic Law Librarianship

Leading Librarians on Teaching Legal Research Skills, Responding to Emerging Technologies, and Adapting to Changing Trends

ASPATORE
BOOKS

Mat #40744686

© 2008 Thomson/Aspatore

All rights reserved. Printed in the United States of America.

Inside the Minds Project Manager, Andrea Peterson; edited by Eddie Fournier; proofread by Melanie Zimmerman

ISBN 978-0-314-19410-7

For corrections, updates, comments, or any other inquiries, please e-mail TLR.AspatoreEditorial@thomson.com.

First Printing, 2008
10 9 8 7 6 5 4 3 2 1

CONTENTS

Seeing the "Whole Elephant": A New Model for Law School Libraries

Paul D. Callister

Director, Leon E. Bloch Library
and Associate Professor of Law

University of Missouri-Kansas City School of Law

ASPATORE
BOOKS

Background: The Factors Shaping My Philosophy of Librarianship

The forces that shape my thinking about libraries differ in degree from many of my colleagues. I graduated from Brigham Young University with a major in philosophy, which has made library and information theory resonate with me. While attending Cornell Law School, I was editor in chief of an international law journal, and from early on I had a deep interest in academic legal writing, particularly with reference to foreign and international law. I practiced law with a small family firm near Los Angeles for nine years, focusing on pension, transactional, and tax law, which tend to emphasize problem-solving and creative thinking skills.

In response to a law school dean who suggested a need for law librarians with an inclination toward scholarship, I eventually pursued a library and information science degree from the University of Illinois at Urbana-Champaign, which grounds its introductory courses in theory, including materials rich in philosophical content. In addition, a flexible curriculum led me to some unusual courses for a librarian—knowledge management, information economics, human-computer interface, and competitive business intelligence. Knowledge management, which stresses what and who an organization knows, rather than physical assets, became a pillar of my management philosophy. I should mention that I never had a class in law librarianship, except an internship at the University of Southern California. This may have been a blessing, since it permitted exposure to a much broader sphere of information science and librarianship.

After graduating, I accepted a position at the University of Illinois College of Law, in part because the university library was the third largest academic library in the country, but also because it had a rigorous promotion and tenure requirement emphasizing scholarship. At the University of Illinois, I was part of a completely new faculty of law librarians under the tutelage of a great director, Janis Johnston. As a result, almost all of us were learning things from scratch. It was a great environment to rethink libraries. I also wrote and published a lot. After three years at the University of Illinois, I was offered the directorship of the law library at the University of Missouri-Kansas City. It was a troubled library, and the law school sought me out because of my scholarship and practice experience, which would help with tenure on the law faculty, rather than years of library and management experience, which were notably lacking on my résumé.

When compared to many of my colleagues who are academic law library directors, I am relatively immersed in scholarship, grounded in legal practice, and lacking long years of library experience, dependent upon a highly articulated philosophy, to guide administration of my library.

Reform in Law School Librarianship: Langdell Is Dead

Academic law librarianship is based on a model created by Christopher Langdell, the dean of Harvard Law School in the late nineteenth century, who believed in the scientific method of law school education. In that model, the library was to be the laboratory,[1] and the mode of teaching was the case method, emphasizing actual appellate cases, to understand the law, rather than traditional legal treatises.

It was a flawed model, in my view, in that it was soon discovered that edited case books are a much better way for students to acquire skills, rather than going to the library to look up the case.[2] Consequently, the law school library role became limited to fringe areas that were not the central emphasis of the law school curriculum. The library supported law reviews and journals, which were its biggest and most demanding patrons, facilitated faculty research, helped with student papers (for the few seminars that required them), and trained students in legal research skills in short, pass/fail courses. Consequently, the library was outside the ambit of 90 percent of law school activity.

Teaching legal research skills to first-year legal students is problematic because they are so distracted by the Socratic method of teaching that it is difficult for a library to compete for the student's attention. The fact that such courses are often pass/fail does not help. Legal writing faculty at many schools have taken over research instruction as part of a first-year legal research and writing program. Sometimes in such courses, research skills are de-emphasized or even relegated to an afterthought compared to

---

[1] See Charles W. Eliot, *Langdell and the Law School,* 33 Harv. L. Rev. 518, 524 (1919–1920).

[2] See Arthur C. Pulling, *The Harvard Law School Library,* 43 Law Libr. J. 1, 3 (1950).

writing. I have surveyed the literature, and there are complaints for the last hundred years about legal research skills among law school graduates and legal research skills courses, including lack thereof, in the curriculum.[3] The one ray of bright hope is upper-level research courses (often focused on particular areas of practice such as litigation, transactional, international, and tax law). In light of the current trend to establish "information literacy" and "lifelong learning" as instructional programs, library colleagues from disciplines other than the law would do well to learn from law's own troubled history with research instruction.

Today, in the modern, electronic information environment, academic law libraries are no longer principally used by students or teachers to "find the law." In most cases, faculty and students utilize electronic databases such as Westlaw and Lexis, and they never leave their offices. It is true that law librarians may teach students and teachers how to use these technologies. They also license the technologies and interface with Westlaw and Lexis about problems with their services, but in large measure, the library has become an invisible portal for research rather than the space where most research activity occurs.

The exceptions with respect to research in the law library are the difficult subjects—interdisciplinary, historical, international, and foreign law research. This is important in collection development. Furthermore, the most valuable asset of the library is its librarians, many of whom must be able to teach as prerequisite to win the confidence of students and faculty.

With respect to research in the library, and following many public libraries, the role of the law school library must shift from being the principle place to "find the law" to becoming a place of intellectual stimulation and a center for self- or group-directed learning. My vision is a library that not only supplements the classroom, but also competes with it as the place of significant learning, offering an alternate method of education.

Finally, in a larger sense, the profession of law needs to remember that it is a "learned profession," and that there are certain values that come from

---

[3] See Paul D. Callister, *Beyond Training: Law Librarianship's Quest for the Pedagogy of Legal Research Education,* 95 Law Libr. J. 7, 9–11 (2003).

reading regularly and being stimulated in the practice of law—values the profession has lost in many respects. Many of today's law students neglect to read the cases they cite in their research. The connection to reading is being lost.

In contrast, going back to England in the seventeenth century, the legal bar evolved around the idea of being a community of readers—that was the essence of legal education. Early English judges and attorneys apparently read Littleton's *Tenures* each Christmas.[4] Furthermore, the life of an English judge in the late fifteenth century was rather contemplative and bibliocentric in nature:

> [T]he justices of England do no sit in the king's courts except for three hours a day, that is, from eight o'clock before noon to eleven o'clock, because those courts are not held in the afternoon... Hence the justices, after they have refreshed themselves, pass the whole of the day in studying the laws, reading Holy Scripture, and otherwise in contemplation at their pleasure...[5]

Indeed, in America, courts even tried to lessen the burden of reading by limiting the number of cases: "The leading lawyers in every State are expected to run over, if they do not read, every case in every new volume of its reports. Every case dropped [from publication] lightens the task."[6] For the last several hundred years, to be a lawyer meant fellowship in a community of readers. The question in my mind is whether academic law libraries can play a role in helping legal education re-emphasize those values.

---

[4] *Westminster Hall or Professional Relics and Anecdotes of the Bar, Bench, and Woolsack* 8 (London, John Knight and Henry Lacey 1825) (describing Roger North as the model law student); see also Gilbert J. Clark, *Life Sketches of Eminent Lawyers: American, English, and Canadian* 101 (Kansas City, Lawyer' International Co. 1895).

[5] John Fortescue, *De Laudibus Legum Anglie* 129 (S.B. Chrimes ed. and trans., Wm. W. Guant & Sons 1986) (1942). The dates ascribed to *De Laudibus Legum Anglia* are between 1468 and 1478. Id. at ix.

[6] Simeon E. Baldwin, *American Judiciary* 274 (1905).

As a final note, there is evidence that law schools are questioning Dean Langdell's model, which has not been updated for over a hundred years.[7] There has never been a better time for law libraries to revise the basic model of the library.

A New Paradigm for Evaluating Law Libraries

I compare my role as a library director to the analogy of the blind man and the elephant—one blind man might see the elephant's trunk as a rope or a hose, and another might see its tusks as a spear, but none see the whole elephant. A library director's job is to "see the whole elephant." With their changing role, law school librarians need to develop new measures, based upon a new paradigm, for evaluating law libraries. The question is "How do I measure a great law library, and how do I know librarians are doing their job?" In thinking about how to manage a library, I use a paradigm with five elements to think about their libraries as the whole elephant and to consider new measurements of success.

Library as Stacks: Proper Consideration of Titles and Volume Counts

First, recognize that a library is made up of stacks that hold vast amounts of materials, and it is important to collect and preserve the right materials. This is the traditional measure of libraries, which has focused on resources. Modern law libraries need to move beyond this narrow view to a broader scheme of evaluation. However, even with respect to these traditional measures, improvements can be made.

In the past, libraries have often focused on the wrong measures of the physical collection: How many volumes does a library have in its collection? Measuring volume counts is really about the sheer size of the collection. However, what volume counts do not reveal is the depth and diversity of a library collection, nor its particular fitness for the law school or institution it serves. For example, if an academic law library has a low ratio of titles to volumes compared to its peers, it means the library's collection mostly consists of large multi-volume sets, many of which may have become

---

[7] See, e.g., *Curriculum Version 2.0*, Harv. L. Bull., Winter 2008, at 17 ("a second generation of the Langdell curriculum is warranted...").

irrelevant because these sets (e.g., case reporters, digests, law reviews, statutory and regulatory codes, and even many loose-leaf treatises) are primarily used on Lexis, Westlaw, and other online services. One of my favorite librarians, Kevin Butterfield, now at William and Mary, once insightfully commented to the effect of, "We emphasize the wrong books. We display the big, pretty sets, when it is the monographs that have become the most relevant." Furthermore, the big sets, reflective of relatively low title-to-volume ratios, do not circulate, but the monographs do. Everything is upside down with respect to what is important in an academic law library collection.

With respect to matching the collection to the law school's priorities and needs, analysis by subject classifications (call number ranges)—how they compare to areas of emphasis, both in number and age—is important. WorldCat Collection Analysis is a new tool that allows a very granular analysis of this kind. Furthermore, it is useful in assessing the inter-library loan capabilities of its local or regional consortium, which for many law schools is essential to facilitating in-depth academic research and the needs of law reviews and journals. Finally, assessment of the broader consortium network students and faculty rely upon raises important questions about the relative number of titles each law library school contributes to local and regional inter-library loan consortia, providing yet another way to measure a collection.

Today, it is important for a library to have materials that stimulate its constituents, that match law school areas of emphasis, that serve interdisciplinary, historical, and foreign and international interests, and that occur primarily in one-volume units. Simply put, a high relative title count reveals good breadth and depth in a collection, its facility for circulation, and its relative contribution to inter-library loan consortia. These are all indications of strength that volume counts by themselves do not detect.

The Library as Portal: Beyond Lexis and Westlaw

A law school library is a portal or window to a much broader world, often through electronic means. Furthermore, many more patrons may visit the library via the Internet than in person. Finally, the library's role as a portal has moved far beyond providing access to Lexis and Westlaw. All of these facets illustrate the library's role as a portal.

Besides Lexis and Westlaw, our library licenses twenty-two databases, not including the several hundred databases accessible through the university library. Since the practice of law is increasingly interdisciplinary, the number of databases is rapidly increasing, which increases the importance of being a great portal. Often these important library roles are overlooked by law faculty and administration, sometimes because of failure to market the databases and relevancy of the library as a portal.

The library's role also involves digitization and electronic content building. Libraries are racing to add rare materials to their collection and digitize their unique holdings. The most visible Web site at the University of Missouri-Kansas City is law professor Douglas Linder's *Famous Trials*, which is supported by the library. The site gets as many as 7 million hits a month. It is important for libraries to spawn and support Web sites that generate this kind of interest and support and market that service aggressively.

The Library as Social Knowledge Network

Law school libraries function as social networks. As mentioned, modern knowledge management is based on the premise that the most valuable asset of any organization is what and whom it knows—not what it owns.[8] Law firms, schools, and libraries have always been based upon that principle, although they have not always acknowledged it. The most valuable thing in a law school library is not its books or databases, but its librarians—what and whom they know. Therefore, cultivating a staff that is plugged into the latest developments in the profession, who are actively engaged in professional and academic organizations, who are networked, and who have established expertise is extremely important.

Furthermore, law librarians need more connection to the legal profession and academia. There is a need for law librarians who can relate to their constituencies as attorneys or scholars. I find librarians with practice experience to be invaluable and something to market. If in teaching roles, they often quickly establish relationships of trust with students.

---

[8] See Carla O'Dell and C. Jackson Grayson Jr., *If Only We Knew What We Know: The Transfer of Internal Knowledge and Best Practice* 3–10 (1998); Alan M. Webber, "Forward: An Economy of Ideas," in Jim Botkin, *Smart Business: How Knowledge Communities Can Revolutionize Your Company* 1 (1999).

Engagement in legal scholarship, academic conferences, and the promotion and tenure process can yield fruitful connections, insights into needed library materials and services, and most importantly, credibility with law faculty and students.

Regardless of the issue of credibility with faculty and students, the changing information environment presents a ripe field of study—copyright and licensing, online censorship, the Patriot Act, freedom of information on the Internet, pedagogy of legal research instruction in digital environments, design of legal information retrieval systems, new methods for evaluating collections, Web site and online tutorial design, best practices in digitization, managing libraries in a changing environment, empirical legal research and how changes in the information environment affect legal institutions, law, jurisprudence, the rule of law, and social stability. Serious research in many of these fields is needed not only for the narrow field of law librarianship, but also for the larger professions of law and librarianship in general.

Sadly, too few librarians are encouraged or have sufficient incentives to develop a serious track of scholarship, since many universities do not have a promotion or tenure process for them. Frankly, many librarians are not interested in scholarship, do not feel they have time for it, and may even resent rewarding those who engage in it.

Library as Impact: Consumption of Legal Information and Library Instruction

A related issue that desperately needs consideration concerns the overall impact the library has on its students, faculty, broader constituency of local patrons, and local inter-library consortia to which it belongs. How much information are the constituents of the law school using? Are law school graduates proficient in legal research skills, especially problem-solving abilities?

My basic premise has always been that the more information my law school uses and consumes, the better. Increased consumption should mean better research among faculty and students, leading to better scholarship. Measuring impact with circulation and reference statistics over time is a start, but the statistics mean nothing without benchmarks for comparisons.

For a variety of reasons, the American Association of Law Libraries and the American Bar Association have elected not to collect and provide the necessary comparative statistics.

For instance, in an informal survey done in 2004 of twenty-five academic law libraries by Blair Kauffman at Yale, the average number of checkouts, excluding items placed on reserves, was 21,505 items. My library had only 1,433. Now, the survey was heavily weighted toward some of the more prestigious law schools, but the extremely low number of checkouts for my library (which placed last) reveals it was not even on the radar with respect to circulation, and by implication, consumption and use of legal information. Similar studies of academic law libraries in Missouri yielded similar disparities on a total and per-student basis. Additionally, not only were circulation statistics poor, but inter-library loan requests initiated by my library were very low. It seemed my constituents were just not using information to the same degree as other schools, at least with respect to physical holdings, but why was that?

Eventually, I noticed there was a direct correlation between the number of titles available per student at each of the law schools in Missouri and their level of inter-library loans. It turned out that the more titles a law school library had, the more inter-library loan requests that library's patrons would initiate for titles from other law school libraries. The implication is that the more information you have, the more you want. From a collection policy perspective, our poor showing in law titles correlated to the relatively low level of interest in requesting titles from other institutions. The library was just not having the impact it needed to stimulate interest and consumption of legal information.

The other important factor besides information consumption is instructional impact. Over the last few years, our law library went from having zero presence in the classroom—which meant librarians could not effectively build relationships of trust and confidence with law students—to offering four different advanced legal research courses. These courses have corresponded to an up-tick in reference traffic.

Because library instructional programs and courses have an impact on building relationships with reference librarians, there is an onus on librarians to always teach well and continually improve their teaching skill. Not every librarian must teach, but each institution must have some librarians who can teach effectively—not just training students, but also educating them.

The distinction I draw between training and education is that training prepares students to be familiar with known information resources and to handle known problems with known solutions, but education facilitates problem-solving skills and prepares students for unknown and unexpected problems, resources, and solutions. A friend of mine, an engineer at Raytheon, a firm with considerable expertise in design of military aircraft, once commented about an airline crash off the West Coast: "The pilot and co-pilot did exactly what they were trained to do, but the plane crashed anyway because they failed to think."[9] Education is about learning to think, not simply perform routine responses to routine problems.

The Library as Place: Communal Forum and Center for Self-Directed Learning

Lastly, the law school library is a communal place that should inspire reverence for the law, communal pride, and a sense of identity. I learned the importance of this principle while attending a Salzburg Seminar on librarianship in the twenty-first century, with participants from all over the world. We adopted a statement on "the vision of the communal roles of law libraries," attached as Appendix A. Although serving as the draftsman, at first it seemed to me that the interest of my colleagues in library facilities and community building had no real application to law libraries. In reality, however, a law school library can play a critical role in providing sanctuary for thought and reflection, in portraying a solemn image of law as a profession and legal education. It can stimulate learning and discovery in a curriculum that has become dry and stale in upper levels and, more ambitiously, in a profession that desperately needs intellectual rejuvenation. It can offer an enticement during recruitment of both faculty and students, and serve as a forum for diverse groups and communities outside of the law school. Although common in public and some university libraries, these are new roles for law libraries.

---

[9] Statement made by Tom Woodall, engineering fellow at Raytheon. See Callister, supra note 3, at 7.

In my own thoughts, Cornell's law library reading room helped shape my identity as a part of that school. In Northern Ireland, a specialty library, the Northern Ireland Political Collection at Linen Hall Library, provides an impartial collection on the subject of the Irish conflict and serves as a communal focal point for reconciliation.[10] From conversations with colleagues at international conferences, I know that in the West Bank and Lebanon, libraries are used as tools to bring youths out of the cycle of violence and provide them with literacy. In a similar fashion, a law school library should be the communal center and intellectual heart of the school.

Almost every law school library has high-tech teaching labs. Unfortunately, many of these technology labs tend to segregate students and encourage independent work, with every student staring at their own monitor, often away from the instructor. At the same time, education pedagogy continues to stress the need for group work and activities as effective instructional methods. Technology is at odds with modern pedagogy. In considering library design as a center for learning, technology labs and classrooms need to realign themselves with modern pedagogy. I find that students often learn online research skills better when working in groups. In preparing for a major facilities upgrade, my library is examining collaborative teaching technologies that permit multiple users to access the same large display and collaborate in research and presentations more easily.

Misperceptions about the Library: Technological Obsolescence and Disintermediation

There is a perception that libraries are technologically obsolete and are being replaced by online search engines—an attitude that often makes it hard to make the case for the resources libraries need. The problem with such reasoning is that it reduces libraries to technologies when in fact they are dynamic social institutions, capable of marvelous adaptation. A library director must always stress the social and organic aspects of his or her organization, and what the library contributes to the community.

Another important misperception is that libraries are succumbing to trends in disintermediation. In the travel industry, this trend means most people

---

[10] See www.linenhall.com/northernIrelandPoliticalCollection.asp (last visited March 31, 2008).

now use the Web to book their vacations instead of a travel agent. Research, it was thought, was now being almost exclusively done in an electronic forum that bypassed the need for human intermediation, such as offered by librarians. However, I see plenty of evidence that human intermediated information services are valued and even increasing their influence. For instance, there is Thomson West's continuing use of armies of lawyer-editors to identify and place points of case law into a taxonomy of more than 100,000 classes and sub-classes. Lexis, which fathered the free-text searching of legal resources, recognized that search algorithms simply did not meet the needs of its clients, and in the 1990s used several hundred attorney-editors to offer a similar intermediated system to compete with Thomson West.

The countertrend toward intermediated services is also evidenced by the continued interest in metadata, by the viability of Yahoo! (the company name stands for "Yet Another Hierarchical Officious Oracle"), which relies on human beings to classify hyperlinks into a taxonomy, and the growth of services such as Wikipedia, which depends upon its own users to intermediate knowledge in a way challenging traditionally established, vetted encyclopedias.

The librarian-educator needs to instill students with the value of intermediated information resources. This is especially true in law because intermediated information systems provide great stability, an essential element of any legal system—"Law must be stable and yet it cannot stand still."[11] It is not just librarianship that depends for its survival upon the perceived value of intermediated information, but it is also the stability of the legal system that may be at stake. Society has a fundamental interest in the survival of intermediated information systems such as those libraries offer.

The Changing Role of Academic Librarianship

Managerial Training for the Next Generation of Law School Librarians

One of the most helpful courses I took in library school, and one I never thought would have any application in my future career, was knowledge

---

[11] Roscoe Pound, *Interpretations of Legal History* 1 (1923).

management. It taught me how to view organizations differently—that the most valuable assets a library possesses are its people, specifically what and whom they know. Sometimes, because of budget constrains or misperceptions that librarians need to spend as much time as possible "at their desks," librarians are discouraged from participating in local, regional, and national organizations. However, for libraries to thrive, they need librarians who network, who learn about best practices, new technologies, and trends, and most importantly, who know whom to call when their own resources and expertise are insufficient. Finally, libraries are fundamentally about sharing and exchanging resources. Again, networking is imperative. Nowhere is this better demonstrated than by the almost honeybee-like instincts and natural capability with which librarians have built vast inter-library loan networks, licensing consortia, and advocacy groups. Those instincts need to be nurtured and rewarded. Those networks also need to be directed into future issues such as collaborative collection development, development of better performance measurements and benchmarks, digitization projects, electronic preservation, digital depositories, and support for open-access publishing.

Law librarians also need to acquire competency in obtaining grant funding and fundraising. Law schools never sought grants in the past, but such funding, especially at state law schools, is increasingly important. In the past, public law schools could function with little financial assistance from their constituent supporters. Now public schools must function as private schools, and library directors are asked to engage in fundraising activities.

Library directors need to learn how to be successful "change agents." My view is that library directors are primarily responsible for establishing an innovative environment and culture where librarians can take pride in their profession, where new ideas are not frowned upon, but rather nurtured, where experimentation is possible, and where professional talent is developed. This is perhaps the hardest task directors face. It requires constant attention, especially when assuming leadership of a new librarian. In the current environment, librarians must be able to adapt rapidly because they need to keep their institutions relevant. For many librarians, this is especially hard because law librarianship was a very stable profession, for at least the last hundred years. That stability was comforting and attracted many to the profession, and now these same individuals are confronted with the need for change. In many cases, a library director will need to call on his or her staff members to do things they have never done before, or even contemplated doing, and in many cases to work with people outside the staff's normal sphere of activity.

One particular trap new directors may fall into in a problem library is that staff may want the incoming director to lay down the law, resolve all disputes, and define everyone's jobs in such a way that there are never any conflicts. This is impossible. Especially in this changing environment, librarians and staff need to understand that they are responsible for helping the institution achieve its objectives rather than focusing on job definitions. They need to work as departmental and cross-departmental teams with the objectives of the library and the institution always in mind. Additionally, when any staff member discovers a problem that interferes with the function of the organization, he or she needs to take responsibility for resolving it and see that it is resolved rather than ignoring it as outside the realm of his or her job. With respect to resolving past disputes, it is usually not necessary to do so, and it may be impossible for a new director to ever find the truth in order to pass judgment on the former problems. It is often much better for the director to get everyone focusing on the future.

Library directors must develop skills in diplomacy, identifying and articulating institutional objectives, and inspiring a vision for staff members to work in teams. Directors must have excellent interpersonal and leadership skills, including getting diverse people to work together. Directors must stress this cooperative culture in assessments and evaluations, one-on-one meetings, and by identifying particular instances of effective teamwork for praise and pointing out specific failures.

Financial Elements of Librarianship: Allocating Resources

The practice of establishing the budget varies from library to library. At some schools, the budget is dictated by the administration using a formula, lump sum, or line item budget, benchmarked against prior years. There are usually opportunities for the director to suggest adjustments or plead his or her library's case. Some schools may even start with a zero budget for their library. In those cases, the library director must justify what the library needs to spend on an annual basis. One of the most important skills a law school library director can learn is the use of incremental budgets. When the dean, faculty, or a potential contributor asks what would the library do with an extra $100,000, the director needs to have a ready answer, based on real numbers, and be able to illustrate how that money would further institutional objectives.

To manage their budget wisely, today's law school library director needs to be involved in the strategic planning of the school. He or she needs to have a thorough understanding of the school's objectives and how the library's collection and services meets those objectives. For example, the University of Missouri-Kansas City School of Law focuses on tax, urban, family, trial, and small business law. As the director of the law school library, I have used those objectives and framed the library's collection development policy after assessing, at a very granular level by using WorldCat Collection Analysis (a new service provided by the Online Computer Library Center), the deficiencies in the library collection. As a benchmark, my library compares its subject holdings (with respect to the school's strategic objectives) to the holdings of the law libraries in its local MOBIUS consortium.

The reasoning is that if the law school has 20 percent of the law students, it should provide 20 percent of the titles with its key subject areas. From the assessment, I know exactly how many titles are needed to carry our weight in the MOBIUS consortium with respect to the school's strategic objectives. I also know how much of my collection is unique relative to items held by only one law school within MOBIUS. This is a measure of what my library contributes to the system that is not replicated elsewhere. My library's collection development policy was then framed based upon the analysis to emphasize those titles that help the library catch up in the areas of emphasis. The WorldCat assessment is also a powerful tool to help the faculty and administration understand the shortfalls in library resources and make the case for more funding in terms of law school strategic objectives.

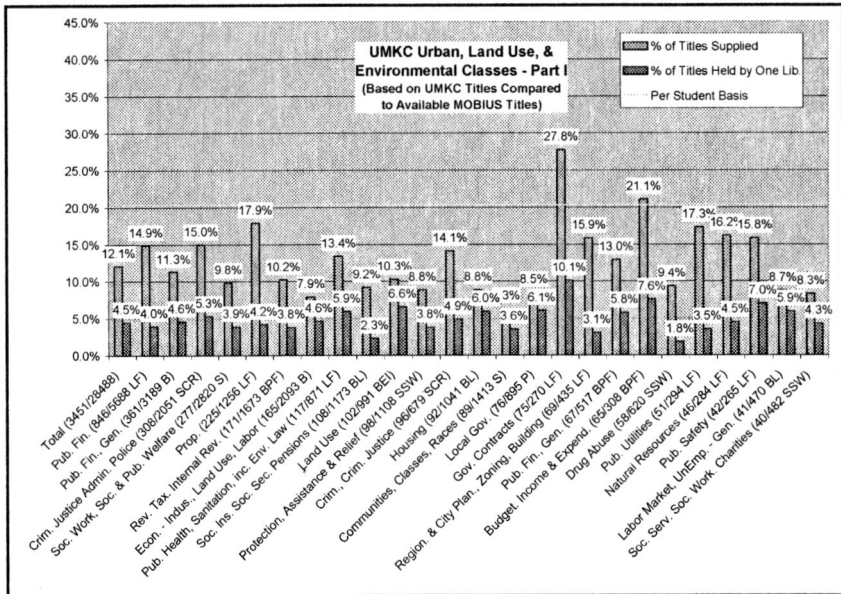

Figure 1: Illustration of Application of WorldCat Collection Analysis

A reality every library director has to face is static budgets, which present real challenges in the face of rapidly escalating costs for serials, which for law libraries mean case and statutory reporters, encyclopedias, and loose-leaf services. Between 1995 and 2007, the average annual price increase for subscription supplementation of multi-volume sets published by Thomson West was around 13 percent.[12] This means even a modest budget increase is really a budget cut. Furthermore, all of the major serial subscription sets are online, and some publishers may be using escalating print prices to drive libraries into the online environment. Even subject-oriented sets, which unlike case reporters have been favored in print, are becoming increasingly usable in online formats. As a result, it is hard to justify keeping them in print.

At the same time, inflation in subscription supplementation costs also tend to eat away at other areas of the collection budget, especially monographs. Again, monographs are important to fill out the diversity and depth of the

---

[12] Kendall F. Svengalis, "Legal Information: Globalization, Conglomerates, and Competition—Monopoly or Free Market" (presentation delivered at the annual meeting of the American Association of Law Libraries, July 15, 2007, New Orleans, Louisiana).

collection, particularly in theoretical, interdisciplinary, historical, foreign, and international subjects. These subject titles largely come from university and academic presses. What is more, these titles circulate, unlike the large serial sets, increasing the library's impact, and a healthy number of such titles make a browsable collection, preserving the need to visit the library. In light of the increasing importance of monographs and the inflationary pressures of subscription serial sets, it is important that librarians fight to fund monographs, which serve the increasingly diverse demands on the collection, and which promote the impact and relevancy of the library.

Communicating Library Services to Students

Another important role a law school library director must play entails building relationships of trust and confidence with law students. To do so, law libraries must have librarians who are credible with students. It is helpful to have librarians who have actually practiced law or have wonderful technology skills. Face time in the classroom is also critical. Otherwise, there is no opportunity to build the relationships leading to student traffic at the reference desk. Having librarians who can instruct, educate, and think in a way students can respond to is a real asset in maintaining the library's relevance.

Bob Berring, formerly the director at Bolt Hall, observed that teaching legal research during the first year of law school is poor timing.[13] During that year, students are so engrossed in their experience with the Socratic method of teaching that an introductory, pass/fail course in research skills tends not to be a priority. Students may not understand the relevance of such a course until the time comes when they have to write papers or start their first jobs or summer clerkships. As a result, research courses offered in the second and third years of law school tend to be more effective. The best way to reach motivated students involves timing of research instruction.

Anything the law library can do to stay relevant to students is important. Student editors of law reviews and journals are likely to be the library's most frequent and demanding customers. Librarians can work on those

---

[13] See Robert C. Berring and Kathleen Vanden Heuvel, *Legal Research: Should Students Learn It or Wing It?* 81 Law Libr. J. 431, 441 (1989).

relationships by providing instructional services, improving inter-library loan services, facilitating difficult requests, and helping with symposium and student note topics. Librarians can also foster relationships of trust by judging moot court or negotiating competitions, working with student clubs and societies, and participating in student events.

Forging Relationships with the Broader Community

Librarians also need to participate in the broader aspects of the university and local communities. It is often easy to slip into focusing only on the law school, but the most successful law school librarians are those who are able to build new relationships outside of their traditional circles. These new partnerships may lead to the acquisition of interdisciplinary databases, professional development opportunities, and avenues to influence university policy in important areas such as information literacy, budgets, security, digital repositories, copyright policy, licensing practices, and information technology services. It is very important to engage the university on a broad level.

An area that needs special attention is relationships with information technology (IT) departments, both at university and law school levels. Often there are strained relations between librarians and IT personnel. Sometimes there is a difference of culture and orientation toward service. Some IT personnel got to where they are by focusing on technological proficiency, sometimes at the expense of developing other important interpersonal and organizational skills. For IT departments, the increasing importance of computer security, issues with copyright liability and licensing, and the fundamental need to have a manageable sphere of responsibility for information technologies all act to create pressures to overlook end users' needs and create locked down IT systems. On the other hand, many librarians, particularly from reference, have a highly developed sense of service, accommodation, and sharing. By nature, they are trained to provide access to information. Conflict is often inevitable. Many of the problems can be resolved through communication. It helps to hire librarians with IT skills who can communicate with the IT department, and when possible to champion the hiring and retention of IT personnel with good communication and interpersonal skills.

My library could not support serious scholarship without a superior inter-library loan system, the elements of which include a union catalog for seventy university libraries across Missouri, catalog links for patron-initiated inter-library loans, a rapid and affordable delivery system, and agreement among participating libraries to provide generous library loan terms (typically a month or semester). Such systems are established and maintained only through networking relationships and professional commitment of librarians from across the state of Missouri to serve on numerous consortium boards and committees. A great librarian must look far beyond the physical and electronic holdings of his or her library to consider the larger information sphere and the benefits of cooperation among diverse libraries.

Besides library and university communities, there are many unexpected benefits from reaching out to potential partners in the community. For example, Kansas City has the second-largest repository for the National Archives and Records Administration (NARA), which is full of legal materials pertaining to federal trials and inmate records from the famous prison at Leavenworth. My law school has faculty members who have conducted research in the area of trial records, but who had never visited or considered the incredible archival resources offered by the NARA. Fortunately, one of my library's research specialists, who was working on her library degree, did an internship at the NARA. Ultimately, the library, the law school, and the NARA hosted a joint symposium that brought together librarians and faculty from various disciplines and NARA archivists from around the nation. Symposium participants saw presentations from different fields on the value of NARA holdings (somewhere on the order of half a million cubic feet of federal trial documents) for legal, historical, and other empirical research. They also discussed threats to those holdings because of the NARA's budgetary constraints. The symposium resulted in a special issue of the law school's law review.[14] That conference not only created new relationships and a buzz about the library, but it contributed to an important national issue affecting academic scholarship.

---

[14] 75 UMKC L. Rev 1–182, 283–332 (2006).

Outside the university, there are many unexpected allies who can enhance the relevancy of a law school library. Actively searching them out must be a priority.

New Technologies: Social Consequences, Instructional Technologies, Pedagogy, and Licensing Issues

In many cases, it is not the technology itself that is most important, but the social consequences of that flow from the technology (e.g., trends in disintermediation, declining student engagement in the classroom as a result of laptops with wireless network capability, student participation as editors on Wikipedia, and faculty enthusiasm for rankings of their downloaded law papers posted on the Social Science Research Network). All of the aforementioned may have consequences for the library, and so simply focusing on mastering technology is never adequate. The library's approach to technology always needs to take into account the social ramifications for the law school of new developments.

I have already mentioned WorldCat Collection Analysis and its facility for in-depth collection analysis. There are many other technologies I could highlight—databases other than Lexis and Westlaw, integrated search platforms, inter-library loan services, library security systems, self-checkout, digital repository software, digitization tools, radio frequency identifiers, patron checkout systems, and so on—but vendors and professional societies do a good job of keeping librarians informed. However, what are often overlooked are instructional technologies and course management systems. Librarians need to master these tools—not just for their own instructional needs, but so they can make the library a dynamic learning center and facilitate the teaching capabilities of the law faculty. Many of these tools may have profound social consequences.

For instance, there are new, collaborative classroom technologies that enable students to work together around a table with one large-screen monitor. Two or more students can be working on that same large-screen display. One student could be doing a search on Lexis and another working with a PowerPoint presentation. Searches of Lexis and Westlaw could be compared side by side. There are all sorts of possibilities. Collaborative technologies are the next wave in legal instruction. In the past, information technologies tended to pull students away from group work, which is reinforced by the Socratic teaching method, reliance on end-of-semester exams as the sole method of evaluation, and class rankings. In practice, however, attorneys have to rely upon collaborative skills and be able to work in teams. The new collaborative technologies have potential to prepare students for the realities of practice, an important social consequence.

With respect to research technologies, librarians need to move beyond training to educate students to recognize and appropriately use intermediated and disintermediated systems, to understand the power and influences of different search algorithms (e.g., natural language versus Boolean), the importance of using field-restricted searching, and how to use reiterative search techniques to take one relevant search result to find the documents that are most similar.[15] It is also important for students to know how to make sure that what they have found is actually good or relevant law, and finally make sure they know how to interpret and contextualize that law correctly through the use of commentary.[16] With information technologies, the temptation is to teach every bell and whistle of the product while forgetting how to make it relevant to the student's research needs and the research process as a whole. The emphasis needs to be on skills and the process of research, rather than products.

The complexity of modern research requires law school librarians to be educators rather than trainers. This is one reason for pulling back from letting Westlaw and Lexis representatives provide all the instruction for electronic research. Research instruction services of vendor representatives should be supplementary to the law school library's efforts. Again, rather than training students on how to use those services as products, librarians need to actively teach research skills and educate students on how to develop their thinking and problem-solving capabilities.

---

[15] See generally Callister, supra note 3.

[16] For a chart of the research cycle, see Appendix B. See also Paul D. Callister, "Thinking about Legal Research Problems: Being Thorough (Completing the Research Cycle)," www.law.umkc.edu/faculty/callister/bootcamp/Survival/tab6.html (last visited March 31, 2008).

Finally, librarians cannot escape the necessity of knowing about copyright and licensing law. It is important to learn how to manage copyright and licensing risks while lawfully continuing library function in the electronic environment. Librarians need to understand who can use the online systems (e.g., walk-in patrons from the community and the local bar), the permissible uses (e.g., academic only or professional), limitations on sharing of bibliographic records supplied by vendors in union catalogs, restrictions on posting or republishing images on the Internet, and inter-library loan limitations (often inter-library loan rights can be authorized per a negotiated license agreement). Posting items in course reserves or in online course management systems can also be problematic.

Navigating the Changing Role of Librarianship: Key Steps

The first step for directors in navigating the changing role of law school librarianship is to take a long, hard look at their libraries. Directors must see the "whole elephant" and know every aspect of their libraries (i.e., the library as stacks, the library as information portal, the library as a social knowledge network, the library as impact, and the library as a source of communal identity and center for self-directed learning). Directors must study their libraries' strengths and weaknesses. This may take considerable time and effort.

In my view, this evaluation is much more important than writing mission statements and action plans. Those statements are overrated as an initial planning tool, especially for new directors. It takes time to understand the mission of a library. Furthermore, such statements tend to mean nothing and provide little guidance if they are too general, and if they are too specific they are insufficiently flexible to encourage pursuit of unexpected opportunities to maintain the library's relevance. I have even heard a librarian or two dismiss a fresh idea as "outside the scope of our mission." However, such opportunities often pop up unexpectedly, and librarians and staff need to be encouraged to respond creatively. For example, law librarians may be called upon to seek grant funding, initiate new digitization projects, teach new courses, and seek out and partner with new community allies. As mentioned, many of the successes my library has enjoyed in recent years have stemmed from building new relationships and then looking out for new opportunities. In addition, directors must understand the law school's strategic plan and objectives, and then build their own based on their understanding of those objectives. For new directors, it is important not to firm up library mission and vision statements until a comprehensive assessment of opportunities and law school objectives has been made.

Following the evaluation stage, it is then important to define the library's mission and go through a planning process with respect to how to address library deficiencies, including a plan that will market the library's relevance based upon the school's strategic objectives. Directors must communicate the library's proposed role in the larger scheme of the law school and what the library's needs are to fully play that role. As a new library director, I had to be able to defend library values and relevancy anytime and to anyone. This is easier to do if the director really knows his or her library and when the relationship of the library to law school strategic objectives has been carefully developed. In this respect, every library needs an articulate spokesperson who has credibility with the faculty and administration.

The final steps of the change process are implementation and assessment. With respect to implementation, the library's culture, already discussed elsewhere, is a key to success. Assessment requires incorporation of the framework discussed above and a feedback loop to ensure a response to deficiencies.

The Importance of Library Routines

Any routines library directors develop with respect to their library staff need to promote a productive and adaptable work environment. Librarians are the most valuable part of any library. Consequently, library directors need to make sure librarians and staff achieve recognition within the law school community at important times (e.g., whenever a librarian gets an educational degree or receives grant funding). It is also important to communicate library contributions and accomplishments with the law school on a routine basis, perhaps through a column in the alumni journal, a weekly newsletter, or periodic e-mails.

With respect to meetings, I have found that routine staff or departmental meetings are often not as important as having regular interviews with every librarian. I try to hold them once a quarter. Librarians and staff appreciate being given the time to talk about their career plans and objectives. Such contact with the director reaffirms their sense of worth.

The director also needs to establish certain routines to reinvigorate him or herself. For me, that comes from learning something new by staying actively involved in the profession and scholarship. Simply stated, the director's focus should remain on establishing routines that help create a dynamic, excited, interested, and adaptable workforce. Everything else will flow from that focus.

Helpful Resources

Librarians are natural resource networkers, because the whole profession is built on a premise of sharing. They love conferences, consortium meetings, and visiting other libraries to see what everyone else is doing. Beyond networking, librarians need to consider paying for outside experts who can identify and define problems and gauge performance benchmarks. When I first became a library director, I did not know much about technical services, so I negotiated, as part of my hiring package, that the law school would pay for a seasoned and well-known expert in technical services to evaluate our library. Admitting gaps in experience and getting appropriate outside help actually tends to build credibility with administrators and faculty, rather than suggest weakness. In another instance, I observed the positive effects of an evaluation of the University of Illinois College of Law's rare book collection by David Warrington, librarian for special collections at Harvard's law library. Warrington confirmed the standing of the University of Illinois's collection as one of the great rare law book collections in the country. This helped clarify the importance of preserving the library's standing, including sufficient funding, among university and law school administrators.

Government Regulation and Enforcement

The primary problem is not overregulation but a decreasing governmental role in regulating access to information resources. Law school libraries are moving from ownership models to licensed access models as they cancel print resources in favor of electronic ones. Static budgets, inflation in print resources, and publisher preferences for electronic media are forcing this change. While library professional literature frequently points out the reality of this shift, the consequences for libraries of relying upon licensing rather than copyright law for access privileges is less understood. In my mind, the key issue is whether libraries can contractually give up privileges they had under copyright law that enabled them to provide services such as circulation, inter-library loans, unrestricted access to images in the public domain, archiving and long-term preservation, and course reserve materials.

In some ways, the library community missed an opportunity to preserve benefits under copyright law in licensing agreements by not adequately considering the benefits of the Uniform Law Computer Information Transaction Act.[17] Although the library community opposed the act, the official comments within the act provided support for consideration of fair use and other privileges as a basis for finding licensing terms to be void as against public policy.[18] For instance, a contractual term prohibiting the use of screen shots of an online service for any reason, including for criticism, comparison between products, and library guides and tutorials, might be voided by courts as inconsistent with fair use privileges under copyright law. Contractual prohibitions restricting archiving of a licensed database, printing documents for classroom use, or supplying inter-library loan requests for selected passages of a work, otherwise protected by fair use,[19] "classroom,"[20] and archival and copying library exceptions under copyright law,[21] might likewise have been voided. The point is that the Uniform Law Computer Information Transaction Act's efforts to create certainty in state contractual law actually would have provided some cover for libraries caught by onerous licensing terms. Now the law is entirely uncertain on the issue.

There are some other important regulator issues affecting academic libraries, but many of them are less of a concern than the general

---

[17] National Conference of Commissioners, Uniform Computer Information Transactions Act (last revisions or amendments completed in 2002), www.law.upenn.edu/bll/archives/ulc/ucita/2002final.htm (last visited March 31, 2008). Only two states have adopted the Uniform act. See Maryland Commercial Law Code Ann. §22–101(2007); Virginia Code Ann. §59.1–501.1 (2007).

[18] See id. at §105, comment 3.

[19] 17 U.S.C. §107.

[20] 17 U.S.C. §110.

[21] 17 U.S.C. §108.

movement into electronic licensing. The three worth mentioning are the problems with "orphan works," works in copyright for which no copyright owner can be located,[22] the problem with the Digital Millennium Copyright Act not providing a fair use exception with respect to liability for circumventing access control technologies (which is in insurmountable barrier for faculty who want the library's help in creating educational video clips from DVDs),[23] and the need to update library exceptions under 17 U.S.C. §108 to permit archiving of items not actually owned by the library, such as material on the Internet, as a part of Internet archiving initiatives.[24] Although important, each of these issues becomes less relevant in a licensed environment.

In summary, the real issue with government regulation is its diminishing role in the face of licensing of electronic media. This has adverse consequences for libraries that rely upon privileges such as fair use to perform many of their functions.

Final Thoughts

If librarians let others define their libraries only as obsolete technologies, libraries will become such. Librarians need to constantly stress the social, communal nature of their organizations—that quality needs to come to the forefront, even in this technological age. While a powerful tool, technology is not the most important aspect of the law school library—it is the social impact of the organization.

The law library profession must abandon Langdell's model and develop new ways to measure libraries using new frameworks that consider physical

---

[22] See "The 'Orphan Works' Problem and Proposed Legislation," statement of Marybeth Peters, the Register of Copyrights before the Subcommittee on Courts, the Internet, and Intellectual Property, Committee on the Judiciary, March 13, 2008, www.copyright.gov/docs/regstat031308.html.

[23] See 17 U.S.C. §1201. Pursuant to the act, the secretary of copyrights is permitted to make exemptions every three years. To date, no exemption has been made for general educational use of content from DVDs. See "Rulemaking on Exemptions from Prohibition on Circumvention of Technological Measures that Control Access to Copyrighted Works," www.copyright.gov/1201/ (last visited March 31, 2008).

[24] See "The Section 108 Study Group," www.section108.gov/ (last visited March 31, 2008).

holdings, the library's portal, networks or expertise, impact, and communal facilities. Librarians serve as dynamic organisms that are capable of marvelous adaptation. Consequently, librarians must be increasingly flexible and willing to change in order for their institutions to stay relevant.

Librarianship is a noble profession. There will always be a place for institutions with fundamental values rooted in sharing, service, and community.

Paul D. Callister is the director of the Leon E. Bloch Library and an associate professor of law at the University of Missouri-Kansas City School of Law. He oversees the administration of all library personnel, operations, and budget for the Leon E. Bloch Library, as well as computer networking and technology support for the School of Law. He also teaches various courses and oversees the law library's informal instructional programs.

Mr. Callister previously served as reference law librarian and assistant professor of library administration at the University of Illinois at Urbana-Champaign College of Law, where he was charged with reference and research, instruction, and Web site design. Prior to that, he was a library intern at the University of Southern California School of Law, where he provided reference and instructional services as part of an internship program while still in library school. Prior to that, he was a shareholder with the law firm of Callister & Callister, where his practice areas included qualified retirement plans, estate planning, business and professional organizations, and transactional law. He also oversaw the firm's computer network.

Mr. Callister earned his B.A. in philosophy from Brigham Young University, his J.D. from Cornell University, and his M.S. in library and information science from the University of Illinois at Urbana-Champaign. He writes and speaks regularly on his areas of expertise, and he has been the recipient of numerous grants and awards.

Acknowledgment: *Thanks to Erin Lavelle, my administrative assistant, for her assistance in editing.*

Evolving Expectations for Law School Librarians

Michelle M. Wu

*Interim Senior Vice Dean for Academic Affairs
and Professor of Law*

Hofstra University School of Law

ASPATORE
BOOKS

The Changing Role

I would argue that many of librarianship's roles (e.g., preservation of information, provision of data or access thereto, instruction) have not necessarily changed in recent years. Rather, how libraries fill those roles has changed dramatically, causing society to view the librarian's roles differently than it has in the past. In addition to those traditional roles, technological advances have created needs where none existed before, and librarians are the most likely candidates to absorb those new roles into their responsibilities in the next decade. Specifically, technology has modified the definition of publishing and authorship, and librarians will find themselves playing a greater role in the authentication of online documents, the selection and storage of online data, and the online publishing of scholarly works.

On why these changes have occurred or will occur, the discussion below will be divided into two subsections: why librarians have altered how they fulfill their traditional roles, and why librarians' roles will likely expand dramatically in the near future.

The Changing Expectations of Existing Roles

Legal education itself is undergoing self-examination and evolution. (See the Carnegie Foundation's *Educating Lawyers: Preparation for the Profession of Law*, published by Jossey-Bass in March of 2007, and the subsequent conferences and workshops on its findings.) The Carnegie report noted that while legal education does an excellent job of introducing students to legal reasoning, it has not successfully exposed students to information or activities necessary for them to transition to the practice of law: skills, ethical responsibilities, social and cultural contexts in which law is enacted, and the different types of legal practice. Therefore, it follows that law libraries, as an integral part of any law school, would undergo a similar transformation. Further, societal and technological changes over the last decade have played their parts in spurring reanalysis and adoption of new service approaches.

The key factors in the changing roles of librarianship are user expectations, changing technologies, and economics. User expectations drive not only what information libraries need to provide, but also in what format. The wide range of user expertise in using legal resources creates challenges in training, to support each user at his or her comfort levels. Technology, of course, affects all aspects of the library, from data storage to delivery to notifying the patron of new developments or services. Economics drive libraries, much as they do law schools, to maximize the services and access to information for users with decreasing resources. Below, each of these factors will be explained in greater detail, often in relation to one another.

In terms of user expectations, we look first to the student. Many of these patrons have been educated in an age of technology, where a classroom without computers is unknown and unacceptable. They are experts (or at least believe they are) at finding data online, and they expect immediate gratification of any need, research or otherwise. Several studies have analyzed students' (primarily undergraduates) research patterns and habits, and each has found that this generation of students has a non-critical view of sources. (See "Perception and Selection of Information Sources by Undergraduate Students: Effects of Avoidant Style, Confidence, and Personal Control in Problem-Solving," Kim, Kyung-Sun and Sin, Sei-Ching, Joanna, 33 *Journal of Academic Librarianship*, 655–65 at page 656, 2007).

For these students, "good enough" is a fine standard. They do not rely on objective data to establish reliability, but instead rely on their subjective sense of the validity of the publication. Accessibility also plays a large role in determining which resources they use, regardless of its reliability or stability. For librarians, this means the traditional instructional role has expanded. Not only do librarians have to instruct students on research methods, but to reach that point, they must first persuade the student to recognize that instruction can be beneficial. Librarians have found various ways to do this, from providing self-help materials (e.g., specialized research guides) or just-in-time instruction (e.g., podcasts) to working more closely with faculty in classes where in-depth research is necessary.

Though students provide the most interesting analysis, faculty and advanced degree students cannot be forgotten. Their expectations may be different from those of J.D. students, but they are no less important in determining how a library fulfills its instructional role. Clearly, there are more information sources today than ever before, and faculty still wants the best source of information, regardless of medium or location of the resource. Technology may not have shaped their educational experiences, but it has changed their expectations in terms of how quickly they can obtain requested documents, and at what cost. They also want to post the information for their students to analyze and discuss. For these users, the librarian's instructional role has expanded in part to include copyright education. While it may be possible to obtain a document immediately and duplicate it at little apparent cost, delays may be necessary because of the need for approvals. The role also now encompasses training on online resources such as TWEN, WebCourses, and Blackboard, tools that may be used to provide relevant documents to students. Though these are not actual research methods, faculty require instruction on (or assistance in) how to distribute research materials effectively, and as such distribution is so closely tied to the reason for the research in the first place, faculty have turned to librarians for assistance in such matters.

Further, all library users now seek more customized services, as they have become familiar with vendor sites such as Amazon, Tivo, and Netflix. While critics question the methodology such vendors use in making recommendations, almost all users have appreciated the extra feature, whether it ultimately proves to be accurate or not. Through such a service, a user may be notified of a title he or she would otherwise have not discovered. This interest in greater customization has appeared in library applications such as the library's online catalog, in the form of self-placed holds and notifications of new titles in user-specified subjects, and so on. And through these tools, the library's role in providing access to information expands to include not only information currently available, but also promising to notify patrons of forthcoming information.

In terms of economics and how this affects the law library's role, one need only look at collections across the nation today. It could easily be argued that collections are becoming more homogeneous. Library budgets cannot keep up with the rate of inflation, as the annual reports on budgeting trends in *Library Journal* show each year. Therefore, even when a library's budget increases, the spending power of that budget typically stays static or decreases. Each year, libraries make difficult choices in collection development and maintenance, and because a law library's core collection is pre-defined (see Interpretation 606-5 of the American Bar Association's

2007-08 Standards for Approval of Law Schools), the monies used to develop the more unique parts of any library's collection are the ones that are most likely to be lost.

Other information resources developments have also affected the law library's collection development role. For example, one of the traditional roles of a library was to develop a collection that would meet the needs of current and future users. However, the increasing number of licensed databases in any library's collection changes this role from building a permanent collection to building current access to data sources.

In all of the examples above, the roles of libraries and librarians have not necessarily changed, but they have expanded.

Future Roles

Moving to the second part of the analysis, the explosion of information sources caused by technological advances (e.g., the Web, decreasing costs for hardware and Web editing software, easier access to high-speed Internet connections) has created needs for information authentication, storage, and retrieval. It has also produced opportunities in publishing for law schools, which could reduce costs and increase publicity/exposure. In each of these areas, law libraries may become key contributors in the development of these new (or rather, more coordinated) services.

In terms of verification, online documents are not as stable as their print counterparts. They can be altered easily; reposted elsewhere with alterations, and removed in a moment. How, then, does a user verify that the document they consulted a year ago is the official, unaltered text? As the American Association of Law Libraries' *State-by-State Report on Authentication of Online Legal Resources* (2007) summarizes, although many official sources can be found online, no state has authenticated online primary legal documents. Access to information is critical, but only if the information is accurate. While governments and authors can provide easy access to information, libraries may need to fill the void of coordinating authentication, for two reasons. First, there needs to be oversight and coordination. While each source could be charged with finding a mechanism to ensure authenticity, this would encourage the proliferation of many methods, and would be no check on the author who decides authentication is unnecessary. Second, librarians, through their work with their users, have recognized the problems caused by unauthenticated data much more quickly than others have. They understand what problems are created by unauthenticated documents (e.g., untrustworthiness and inconsistencies), as well as what practices would most likely cure these problems.

Storage of online scholarly publications is another area likely to fall within the law librarian's future roles. Many libraries already support a print archive, and most universities provide some sort of online archive. However, many scholars at those universities have not yet become accustomed to depositing their works with these archives. As law journals and publishing generally move closer to born-digital publications, this gap will likely close. At that time, schools and their libraries will need to develop sophisticated ways not only to store information, but also to publish, organize, and retrieve it. Again, why libraries? Because librarians are most familiar with the manner of use of information and how patrons expect or want to retrieve such information. This particular role will likely be a shared one, between the university's information technology department and the library. The information technology department should provide the storage, while the library provides the organization. The two will work together on publishing and retrieval.

Last, as data on the Web continues to grow, libraries will seek new ways to organize it. While search giants have used directors and engines to make searching easy, these do not necessarily produce the best results. It is possible that a joint effort by law libraries will create a virtual law library, where none of the data necessarily resides in a single place, but libraries would combine their organizational and authentication roles to produce a virtual subset of Web data for legal researchers. This would make it simpler for those seeking legal information online to identify valid sources, and to limit their searching accordingly. While individual law libraries have made such attempts in the last few years, a coordinated effort would much more likely be successful.

Current Trends

Given these factors, how have law libraries and librarians responded to the trends that are facing them? In terms of services, libraries are looking to provide greater customization (e.g., saved preference lists and notifications through integrated library systems) and more education (e.g., specialized research instruction, such as what is needed for seminar papers). More broadly, they continue to seek ways to evaluate resources in terms of validity and reliability, and to inform their users of such analysis; engage in the preservation of deteriorating and digitally born information in portable formats; and develop cooperative arrangements for collection development, storage, and retrieval. These latter three goals have always existed, but changing technology has added significantly new challenges.

Libraries have always had networks and rely on each other to provide services (e.g., inter-library loan, consortia agreements), but we are seeing greater collaboration not only between academic libraries, but also between private and academic law libraries. The partnership between academic libraries is natural and necessary. As resources become more costly and space becomes scarce, libraries are seeking ways to maximize their resources by entering into collaborative storage and/or retention agreements. For example, some libraries have entered into collaborative storage agreements, where the members within a consortium divide up responsibility for retention and maintenance of certain titles (e.g., one library stores and makes available to other member libraries journals with titles ranging from A to C, stores and makes available to other member libraries journals with titles ranging from D to F, etc.). In such instances, the libraries together must work carefully to define the parameters of the project and any restrictions on the participating libraries (e.g., the library may not discard journals with titles from A to C without written agreement from the other participating libraries).

The relationship between private and academic law libraries is similarly growing. As the Carnegie Foundation and other sources (see *The New York Times*, "When Rendering Decisions, Judges Are Finding Law Reviews Irrelevant," Adam Liptak, March 19, 2007) have pointed out, one criticism of legal education is that it is becoming too removed from the practice of law. Similarly, law libraries teach research skills, but firm librarians find new associates inadequately prepared for research in practice. Therefore, law firm libraries and academic law libraries are partnering to ensure that the research education provided to students in law school will correspond to the skills they will need as summer associates or as graduates. Presently, there are various "bridging the gap" programs across the nation, but these have not reached a sufficiently broad number of students yet. The academic law libraries and the private law libraries special interest sections of the American Association of Law Libraries are working together this year to survey their memberships in order to create a better research education program for law students.

Libraries are also seeking greater collaboration between libraries and other industries (i.e., the Open Content Alliance). The Boston Library Consortium recently announced that its nineteen member institutions would all contribute to an effort to digitize and make publicly available public domain documents within their collections (see the press release at www.blc.org/news/blc_oca_release.html). By harnessing the strengths of each organization, libraries and their partners can provide society and their patrons with the best service possible with a minimal duplication of effort.

Essential Skills

While various technical skills are certainly needed by law librarians, since technology changes so rapidly, that listing of skills would be outdated almost as soon as it was put into print. Flexibility and creativity, therefore, are the two skills that are most necessary to the librarianship role. Libraries are service organizations, and they must adapt to what their users need or likely will need in the future. Flexibility will allow librarians to adjust current practices and services as needs change, and creativity will allow them to make educated guesses on future needs and take calculated risks to fill them.

Librarians must also be skilled marketers of their libraries' services. Ask any librarian how they market their library's services, and you may get as many answers and ideas as there are libraries. Librarians use any marketing source available, whether it's a printed newsletter, e-mail, instant messages, blogging, or an RSS feed. They will create bookmarks for their students for inclusion in orientation sessions, conduct tours, create display cases, and work with other law school departments to disseminate information about the library. They will work with professors in specialized areas to announce customized research instructional sessions, or to create research guides just for those classes. They will guest lecture or co-lecture on research topics. For alumni and the practicing bar, librarians may work with the local bar association or post notices in their school's alumni magazine.

The Importance of Marketing and Communication

It is extremely important for law school librarians to effectively communicate the library's services for two reasons. First, where information is plentiful, it is easy for users, particularly students, to overlook the library and the librarian in their quests for information. As a simple Google search can pull up numerous documents on a given topic, this is frequently where the search ends, even if much more valuable information on the topic is available elsewhere. The library is capable of providing so many services to assist the user—from creating customized clipping queries, to instruction, to training research assistants—that it has failed in its primary function if it has not made users aware of its services.

Second, a smoothly running library is easy to overlook. Without constant marketing and explanation, a law school may forget about the library when a giving opportunity presents itself, or may not understand the consequences of cutting a library's budget. By remaining relevant to its primary user base, a library will ensure that it is recognized and remembered when key decisions need to be made.

Traditional communication techniques (e.g., e-mails, newsletters), as previously mentioned, are still used. However, with faculty and administration, full involvement in the life of the law school and constant in-person communication are the most effective marketing tools. Administrative department heads may rarely seek out a library, since it may not occur to them that a library's services can benefit them in any way. Therefore, it is the library's responsibility to monitor department projects, and to offer assistance where appropriate. By bringing attention to the instances in which the library can assist, departments will learn more about the library, and will start to involve the library in their own endeavors.

Communication or marketing mistakes can best be avoided by knowing your users, and how best to communicate with them, and by being willing to adapt or try new marketing methods as needed. Most important, you need to know your users, and what parts of their responsibilities might benefit from a librarian's services or expertise. The only way to gain this knowledge is to remain in constant communication with those users.

Valued Services

The library services that are most valued by today's law school students include reference assistance, online access to information, and space.

The students who use the library's services most are usually those who "discover" a reference librarian during their first year of law school, typically when they are working on an assignment in their first-year legal research and writing class. Those who have attempted to do the assignments on their own, have failed, and then have approached a librarian, quickly recognize that seeking assistance can often result in more efficient searching. Once that initial discovery is made, students will return throughout their law school years (and after) to seek out assistance. Unfortunately, as discussed below, the most difficult task for the library is to make students aware of their librarians and encourage a willingness to ask them for assistance.

Since students are much more comfortable with online searching than any other type, students also appreciate access to online databases, especially after they graduate and find out how much the services cost in practice. The ability to learn and practice searching these databases while in law school is invaluable. Although librarians would be overjoyed if patrons appreciated resources in other media half as much, it is true that students primarily appreciate the ones that are easiest to access on-site and remotely.

The provision of space, particularly quiet study space, remains important for students. They need areas in which to study individually and collaborate with groups. They also seek social areas, both inside the library and outside. Debate continues on whether this space need be inside a library, and the answer is that it probably does not, as long as it is close to research sources. With online databases and remote access, this is now possible.

Challenges for Law School Librarians

There are several messages that may be difficult for law school librarians to get across, including the fact that the librarian can assist the student in research, and that strong research skills will ultimately benefit them greatly in practice. Despite introducing librarians during orientation or in a legal research and writing class, many students fail to remember that librarians can assist them in their research.

This is partially because this is a self-help generation, and because there are few tools in law school to prepare students for the reality of practice. With so much information online, it often appears that the answer a student is seeking is only a click away. With students' generous access to databases such as Lexis, Westlaw, BNA, and others, they often do not learn to value the well-crafted search or distinguish between sources. After all, they do not pay the licensing bills, and in law school, they have the leisure to scroll through a few hundred cases if they choose. In real life, the case load and the costs of research make apparent the benefit of strong search skills.

No matter how librarians have tried to imitate life after law school, through providing assignments or cost sheets to students, the lesson that research skills are valuable is something students must learn in practice. It cannot be adequately simulated.

Managerial Training and Career Trajectories

Similarly, the types of managerial training most necessary for law library management in the years to come may not be something that can be taught in a classroom. Aside from the usual training in supervision, leadership, and budgeting, future law library managers need to be savvy political players, marketers, and fundraisers. They need to be involved in politics, as the constituents of libraries may have widely ranging needs, often in apparent conflict with each other. To prioritize, or to explain to a particular constituency why a project needs to be placed on hold or cannot be undertaken at all, a librarian must be aware of all options and their costs (financially and in terms of goodwill). Marketing, as discussed above, is also an essential function of the library, to ensure that the personnel and collection of the library are consulted by the population they are intended to serve. Last, as costs increase, a library director must also seek ways to raise funds, as inflation will almost always outpace any reasonable budgetary increases. Special projects or collections may well depend entirely on such efforts.

At the same time, the opportunities for law librarians are greater now than they have ever been. Not only may they stay in libraries, but they may also move to the information technology sector. Most technology-savvy companies recognize the important organizational skills of librarians, and can put them to good use (whether in designing mechanisms to store, order, and retrieve data, refining research methods or creating new research tools, or training others to research more effectively and efficiently). Further, because library directors supervise staff and manage budgets, they are seen as capable and thoughtful administrators in any arena, inside or outside of libraries. Even law schools have recognized the superior organizational skills of their librarians, as lately a number of librarians have been persuaded to take on non-library decanal or administrative positions within the law school, even after they have expressed a desire to retire.

Final Thoughts: Looking to the Future

For librarians to better prepare their patrons for coming technologies in legal research, they need to work more closely with law firms as well as the legal writing and skills departments at each school. They should also seek out news sources on technology developments in law practice, information delivery, and storage. Where appropriate, they should provide education to their patrons about these upcoming services, and illustrate how they could be used to the patron's advantage.

In the years to come, I believe law school librarians will thrive so long as they continue to be open-minded and flexible. Libraries are changing, and user expectations will continue to evolve and expand. We can help to create the future information society, or we can make libraries obsolete. I believe our core roles remain the same, but we must be receptive to filling them in different ways, and in seeking out related roles that logically tie into the traditional roles.[1]

---

[1] For a history of law librarianship, see Brock, Christine A. "Law Libraries and Librarians: A Revisionist History; or More Than You Ever Wanted to Know." *Law Library Journal* 67 (1974) 325–61, and Bob Berring's "Brief History of Law Librarianship" in *Law Librarianship in the Twenty-First Century* (2007). Please also see the ALL-SIS Marketing Toolkit (www.aallnet.org/sis/allsis/toolkit/index.asp). While somewhat dated, it still provides useful information to librarians with questions about how and why to market their libraries.

Michelle M. Wu is presently the interim senior vice dean for academic affairs and a professor of law at the Hofstra University School of Law. She is also the permanent law library director of Hofstra's law library. Prior to her appointment at Hofstra, she worked for both the George Washington University's law library and the University of Houston's law library in various capacities, ranging from government documents/reference librarian to computer services librarian to acting director.

Ms. Wu has authored or co-authored articles on government contracting law, copyright, library personnel management, and access services. She presently serves as the chair of the academic law libraries special interest section of the American Association of Law Libraries and is a member of the association's committee on libraries and technology.

A New Law School Library and a New Role for Librarians

Philip C. Berwick

Associate Dean, Information Resources

Washington University in St. Louis School of Law

ASPATORE
BOOKS

An Overview: Role of the Law Library

The two missions of the law school have always been: (1) the transmitting/imparting of knowledge and skills to students who intend to practice law, and (2) the creating/producing of knowledge—in other words, the teaching/training and research functions. The law library has always played a central role in assisting the law school in achieving these two missions, because students needed access to those materials that would help them learn the law, and faculty needed access to materials that would support their research endeavors. At the beginning of the twenty-first century, these missions remain the same.

The importance of the law library is recognized by the national accrediting agency, the American Bar Association's (ABA) section of legal education and admission to the bar. In its 2007–2008 *Standards and Rules of Procedure for Approval of Law Schools*, Chapter 6, "Library and Information Resources," details six standards a law school has to be in compliance with in order for it to be accredited. Chapter 7, which deals with law school facilities, contains Standard 708, which deals with the law library's physical plant.

The ABA standards make it clear that in order for a law school to succeed in its dual missions, it must have an adequate library collection. ABA Standard 606(a) sets some minimum collecting level by broadly defining a core collection. "The law library shall provide a core collection of essential materials accessible in the law library." Interpretation 606-5 defines the core collection referring to both federal and state primary materials. Some examples in this group include all federal court decisions and reported decisions of the highest appellate court of each state, federal codes and annotated codes for each state, federal administrative codes, and the administrative code of the state in which the law school is located. A number of secondary materials are enumerated, including congressional materials, "significant secondary works necessary to support the programs of the law school," and various indexes and citators. ABA Section 606(b) sets out collection requirements beyond those "essential" core titles. Section 606(b)(2) and (3) specifically state that the law library shall provide a collection that "supports the teaching, scholarship, research, and service interests of the faculty" and "serves the law school's special teaching, scholarship, research, and service objectives." (2007–2008 ABA Standards, p. 44)

These collecting standards accurately reflect the bifurcated goal structure of the law school. Part of the collection must be composed of primary materials such as statutes, cases, and administrative rules and regulations, which are heavily used in legal research and writing programs. As a result, the composition of this core part of the library collection would be similar from school to school. However, the library also contains a large number of secondary materials. While some of these materials are considered part of the essential core collection—law treatises and law journals, and practice materials, for example, to be used by students—many secondary materials are used by faculty to pursue their intellectual agendas. For example, a collection might contain a substantial Chinese law collection of several thousand volumes, many of which are in the vernacular and have been developed over a long period to support the research agenda of a number of faculty who are experts in Chinese law. Thus, the law collection often reflected these individual intellectual pursuits or specific school-wide endeavors, which resulted in certain law schools being known for having strengths in specific law or law-related areas beyond what you would expect to find in a typical law library.

In addition to providing general standards regarding the library's collection, ABA Standard 605 states that, "a law library shall provide the appropriate range and depth of reference, instructional, bibliographic, and other services to meet the needs of the law school's teaching, scholarship, research, and service programs." Interpretation 605-1 fleshes out the standard with a list of appropriate services that includes reference, access (including cataloging), inter-library loan and document delivery, enhancing the research and bibliographic skills of students, and producing library publications. These services provide the basis for the organizational scheme of the law library. This is the scheme that essentially remains in effect today.

The staffing of the law library has typically reflected the need to get bibliographic and physical control over an extensive paper format collection, and the need to provide research and teaching support through the use of this collection. Large numbers of staff were required to ensure that materials were properly acquired and catalogued. The physical collection had to be kept up to date, and the library itself had to be maintained. In addition, a core group of highly trained and educated professionals was needed to assist in the faculty's research endeavors, support the school's legal research component, and provide ready reference services to patrons. These professionals often became specialists. The government documents librarian, foreign and international law librarian, and rare book librarian are three examples specialty areas that are found in many law libraries. It is also important to note that the public services librarians often were not active participants in the law school's research and writing program in the sense that they taught the research component on a regular basis. For the most part, professional library staff really provided ad hoc instructional services to students in the form of walk-up inquiries by students at the reference desk as students worked their way through research assignments, open memos, or briefs.

Technology Affects the Law Library

Starting in the mid-1980s, this paper-based model, which had existed for decades, began to erode. Newly introduced computer technologies rapidly automated many of the basic library record-keeping activities. In addition, full-text online databases such as Westlaw and Lexis matured and expanded, making primary materials available in electronic format. As these databases matured, they continued to add many more titles and soon contained many thousands of titles in electronic format. Also, during the last five years most loose-leaf services have published online versions of their paper products. Moreover, large microform sets have been republished in PDF format. In addition, many law reviews are now published directly on their law school's Web site, and the traditional academic publication cycle has been altered with the advent of the Social Science Research Network (with its Legal Research Network component) and electronic publishers such as Berkeley Electronic Press, which produce peer-reviewed electronic journals.

The change from paper to electronically formatted publications mirrored the rapid adoption of computer technology in other areas of academic life. Most law schools now require their students to own laptops, classrooms are wired for projection and recording capabilities, and law schools are wireless. These changes, in turn, have influenced how the law library is viewed by its major patrons—faculty and students. No longer do faculty members have to venture into the stacks to retrieve journal articles. Nor do students have to wander into the library to make use of a computer lab, or go to a reference desk to ask for assistance at the reference desk.

It has been argued that with the rapid growth of full-text online sources, the law library is no longer the central repository for information and, as a result, is no longer an indispensable resource supporting the law school's two missions. Many law librarians have concluded that the library's reduced role has resulted in recent changes in Standard 603 of the ABA, which describes the educational, knowledge, and job status requirements of the library director.

Prior to 1999, Standard 603(d) stated that, "The director of a law library holds a faculty appointment." From 1999 onward, Standard 603(d) was changed to read, "Except in extraordinary circumstances, a law library director shall hold a faculty appointment with security of position." Recently deans have seized on this language to hire directors outside of the traditional law professor tenure track. This shift can also be tracked in the Association of American Law Schools handbook. The 2003 edition states in Section 6-10 of its bylaws that, "a member school shall have a full-time librarian and a staff of sufficient number and with sufficient training to develop and maintain a high level of service to the program. The director of the library should be a full participating member of the faculty." The 2004 edition of the handbook leaves out the second sentence (Section 6-8). Sections were renumbered, and the bylaws now merely address sufficiency of staff.

In the 2005–2006 edition of the ABA Standards, a new standard was added to the facilities chapter. Standard 704 describes in very broad terms the technological capacities that must be found in accredited law schools. It is interesting to note that this change put much law school technology clearly outside of library operations, further emphasizing what is perceived to be the reduced role the library plays in this important area.

To conclude, for decades libraries and librarians played a major role in the intellectual life of the law school. Their importance was largely based on the library being the repository for print materials, requiring students and faculty to go into the library to find relevant information. As the transition has occurred from print materials to online materials, a case can be made that the library's importance in terms of the dual missions of the law school has diminished. As the need to physically go into the library has been reduced, law schools are examining the need to maintain library staffing levels, and in some instances they have even suggested that the number of professional staff can be reduced. The question is how can law librarians answer this challenge?

Responding to New Technology: A New Teaching Role

It is clear that the role of the law library in the law school setting is undergoing scrutiny largely as the result of rapid changes in information technology. To remain an active force within the law school, the law library must be "meaningfully integrated" into the intellectual life of the law school (article by Michael J. Slinger, 83 *Law. Libr. Journal* 685, 1991). To be meaningfully integrated means the law school community recognizes that the law library plays an indispensable role in helping the law school achieve its educational mission (paraphrasing Slinger at 690–691). What are some of the indicia of this recognition? One is that the activity level of the law library is high. There are in-house publications, many training sessions, expanded research services for faculty and students, and the library plays an active role in the school's research and writing program. Secondly, librarians actively participate in the governance of the law school. They are members of the law school committees and participate in both formal and informal faculty gatherings. For example, librarians are members of the admissions committee and have membership on the curriculum committee.

In other words, today's law library must be an active force in the law school community. Otherwise, they will be looked upon as a drain and not an asset to the law school's educational program. The information revolution provides law libraries with the opportunity to reevaluate and reconstitute themselves so they are indeed "meaningfully integrated" into the intellectual life of the law school. A number of studies and reports have concluded that the traditional law school curriculum should be altered to include many more practical/skills courses. As discussed below, these reports support the case for law librarians being active participants in the intellectual life of the law school.

In 1992, the ABA's section on legal education and admissions to the bar released a report written by the Task Force in Law Schools and the Profession: Narrowing the Gap entitled "Legal Education and Professional Development: An Educational Continuum." Part II of this report, "A Vision of the Skills and Values Which New Lawyers Should Seek to Acquire," states that, "in order to conduct legal research effectively, a lawyer should have a working knowledge of...the fundamental tools of legal research..." In the commentary section, the report states, "It can hardly be doubted that the ability to do legal research is one of the skills that any competent legal practitioner must possess." (p. 163) It is clear that the practicing bar places high value on the ability to conduct high-quality legal research.

More recently, two publications reinforce the need for skills training in legal research as part of a core law school curriculum. The first, *Educating Lawyers: Preparation for the Profession of Law*, by William M. Sullivan, Anne Colby, et al, states in the introduction that "we explore the modes of teaching and learning that law schools use to accomplish the common aim of all professional education: specialized knowledge and professional identity." (Sullivan, p. 3) Echoing the premise of the 1992 report (discussed above), this report identifies legal writing courses as one area that can emulate an apprenticeship through a simulated practice environment. The second publication, *Best Practices for Legal Education*, by Roy Stuckey and others (CLEA, 2007), also proposes changes in law school curricula so "they can most effectively prepare students for practice" (p. 1).

What is clear from these publications is that the practicing bar has concluded that law schools ought to provide more skills training to students so they become effective lawyers more quickly than is now the case. It is also clear the practicing bar places a high value on knowledge of legal research materials and the skills to use them, for these are identified as core skills. Based on their training and experience, law librarians are aptly suited to introduce students to the legal research process. They are also the best people to teach students how to use the different types of legal research materials available through publishers' Web sites, such as the Bureau of National Affairs, Commerce Clearinghouse, and Hein OnLine, and not just those titles through the big aggregators such as Westlaw and Lexis.

Most law librarians have a unique perspective regarding research, since many are both lawyers and librarians. First, because law librarians use a myriad of legal materials every day, they are knowledgeable about all the different kinds of legal resources available and when to use them. Second, because they use these materials on a daily basis, they are able to expertly instruct students on how these various types of materials are used in a research plan. Third, because they keep up to date on changes in information technologies by attending professional meetings, subscribing to list serves, reviewing blogs, and so on, they can quickly and expertly respond to students who have questions regarding new online sources. For example, most law librarians receive monthly newsletters from HeinOnline that announce new publications and changes to its Web site. Fourth, because many are lawyers, they understand the process of legal problem-solving—legal analysis. Thus, because of their unique expertise on how collections are organized—not withstanding format—they can provide an understanding of the most appropriate use for each of these specific resources in the research process.

Working with Students and Faculty

Every law school has a required introductory course in legal research and writing. The professional librarians should play a role in this course. The ideal role would be for the librarians to teach some sort of research component that is assigned a separate grade. This component could either be part of the writing course/program or even a separate course. The benefits of having the librarians actively participate in this course are many. Most importantly, students from day one see the librarian as an expert in the field who is comfortable with both traditional and online sources. In addition, because most of these types of courses are taught in the small section format with much interaction between student and instructor, the students often use the instructor/librarian as a reference for summer employment or even as a reference for clerkship opportunities.

In addition to participating in the first-year legal programs, the professional library staff should be providing assistance in upper-level classes. Some sort of advance legal research course should be taught. This course goes far beyond the basic materials found in the first-year research courses, and seeks to expand the students' awareness of materials that are valuable to everyday transactions practice. For example, students in the advanced legal research course have several sessions on finding public records. These sessions explain how publicly available information like online phone books and MySpace can be used, and they discuss how to gain access to public information filed with the government such as voter registration, licensing lists, and real property data. There are also sessions by vendors such as Westlaw and Lexis who provide demonstrations of people-finding databases that are not available to students. Students are also introduced to various aggregators of statistical reports that could assist them in gathering information about industries or the economies of various geographical entities. In addition to making students aware of the number of online sources available, an advanced legal research course also teaches students how to evaluate these online sources.

Law librarians also are a valuable asset in providing bibliographic instruction to students in seminars and other advanced writing courses. For instance, in a course dealing with antitrust law in Europe, the law librarian would introduce students to foreign legal materials—materials that deal with supranational organizations such as the European Community—and Web sites on which these materials can be located, such as GlobalLex, an electronic database maintained by the New York University School of Law that is dedicated to international and foreign law research. Librarians could also assist students in researching paper topics, acting as both a research adviser and an instructor. It is particularly important that librarians actively participate in these courses, because not only do they know of the existence of many online legal research Web sites with which students are not familiar—the Virtual Chase is but one example—but they also have experience using databases like Thomson's "Web of Science" database, found on the university's main library Web site, that might assist students in a given topic.

Outside of the formal classroom setting, librarians can also assist those students who participate on law reviews. In this instance, the assistance takes the form of training students on both how to best use the technology to research their respective journal topics, and how to use technology to their advantage to efficiently cite-check submitted articles. Finally, librarians can utilize their information professional skills to assist law review staffs develop an effective intranet, making use of technologies to organize and store cited materials found in submitted articles.

Librarians can also become "super" researchers for faculty for many of the reasons listed above. However, in this instance, the librarian acts as a consultant to the faculty member and provides expert advice on how to gather information for a specific research project. It must be emphasized that librarians are not to be the main contact point for routine requests for information, such as, "Does a treatise exist on a particular subject?" or "Have there been any recent periodical articles written on this topic?" These types of requests are to be handled by student research assistants or reference desk staff. The librarian is a collaborator who, through the reference interview process and their knowledge of the bibliography in a given area, is able to assist the faculty member in their research agenda to an extent that is not possible by someone not well versed in the bibliography of the field nor technologically proficient.

Finally, librarians are or should be the experts on technologies that can be of assistance pedagogically. They can suggest when it is appropriate to use RSS feeds, podcasts, webcasting, blogs, and wikis in a given classroom setting. If any of these technologies is adopted, the librarian can assist in it being implemented. Blogs and wikis in particular appear to be prime candidates to be incorporated into a particular class. For example a professor can maintain a torts blog for their torts class. This blog would be part of the law school's intranet and thus available only to students in the class. Professors can have an active class wiki in which students actively participate. If the law school has a robust intranet, both the wiki and blog pages could appear as part of the course page template. On a more global level, librarians should be part of the law school's technology development team, providing needed leadership in this rapidly changing area. They are the ideal candidates to evaluate technology in terms of its ease of use and whether it adds value to the educational mission of the law school.

There are many ways law librarians can market these services to faculty and students. Librarians can send out global or directed e-mails to students advertising mini-lessons or an end-of-year refresher open to all before the summer break. General announcements can be made on the law school's intranet or in the school's daily electronic newspaper. Librarians can reach out to faculty by e-mailing them, distributing brochures, or directing faculty to the law library Web site where a description of professional research services is located. In addition, librarians can schedule regular presentations to faculty on new electronic subscriptions or have more focused help sessions on how to use newly acquired databases. Librarians can also market in an indirect manner by participating on law school committees and attending law school functions. For example, at some law schools, while the librarians always offered bibliographic instruction to seminars, they did not actively participate in the first-year research and writing program. After the director of the law library began a well-received advanced legal research class. This, in turn, led to the professional staff being asked to teach in the legal writing program. Finally, this led to the research component being separated out from the writing course (although the librarians still teamed up with writing instructors) and being taught as a graded one-credit course. The librarians received lecturer titles and teaching stipends.

Conclusion

In a recent article, "A Strategy for Academic Libraries in the First Quarter of the Twenty-First Century," David W. Lewis, dean of the University Library at Indiana University-Purdue University, describes a model that takes into account the enormous increase in digital content and the maturing of the Internet, and what changes have to occur for the library to remain an active force in the academy (http://hdl.handle.net/1805/953). One of his planning assumptions is that "real change requires real change. Incremental adjustments at the margins will not suffice; rather alterations in fundamental practice will be needed" (http://hdl.handle.net/1805/953 at 3). Of the five components to his model, one calls for the repositioning of library and information tools, resources, and expertise "so that they are embedded into the teaching, learning, and research enterprise" (http://hdl.handle.net/1805/953 at 1).

This text has shown that the main missions of the law school have not changed, even though digital/computer technology has been incorporated into all activities in the legal academy, including law libraries. It has also shown, following Lewis, that as law libraries seek to reposition themselves so they remain a central part of law school life, law librarians should play an ever-growing role as teachers. Academic law librarians should take advantage of this time of change and place themselves squarely into one of the basic missions of the law school: the training of students to be lawyers. However, I believe to have the best chance at remaining relevant, academic law librarians must teach a separate legal research course in the first-year program and teach an advanced legal research course. Just incrementally increasing their teaching duties will not suffice.

Will academic law librarians successfully achieve this goal? It is not certain. Nevertheless, I think law librarians will succeed since they possess a unique combination of legal and technical knowledge, research skills, and technical skills. With these requisite skills, they will reposition themselves so they can play an important role in the law school's intellectual life, thus actively contributing to the training and research missions of law schools for years to come.

Philip C. Berwick is the associate dean for information resources and a lecturer in law at the Washington University School of Law in Saint Louis. He previously served as the director of the law library at George Mason University School of Law, as the assistant law librarian for public services at the Georgetown University Law Center, as the head of the law library reading room at the Library of Congress, as an associate law librarian and visiting assistant professor of law at the University of Toledo College of Law, and as an evening circulation clerk at the University of Toledo College of Law.

Mr. Berwick is involved with the American Bar Association, the American Association of Law Libraries, the Capital Consortium Network, the Law Librarians' Society of Washington, D.C., the Mid-America Association of Law Libraries, the Ohio Bar, the Ohio Regional Association of Law Libraries, the Southeastern Association of Law Libraries, the Thomson West academic advisory board, and the Virginia Association of Law Libraries. He has been the editor of Trends in Law Library Management and Technology *since 2002. He earned his B.A. from the University of Pennsylvania, his J.D. from the University of Toledo College of Law, and his A.M.L.S. from the University of Michigan School of Library Science.*

Dedication: *I dedicate this chapter to Carol, who has always supported me no matter what the cost to her.*

Acknowledgment: *I also gratefully acknowledge the assistance of Carol Ann Fichtelman Esq. in the editing of this chapter.*

Skills and Concerns of Future and Continuing Academic Law Librarians

Nancy L. Strohmeyer

*Associate Director and Head of Public Services
and Associate Professor of Law Library*

Barry University School of Law Library

People outside of the library field sometimes ask me if I believe there will be a need for librarians in the future. I consider this question insulting and fairly ignorant, because it presumes that librarians are all the same and that they are unable to change. It is also based on the stereotypical image of the librarian as someone who knows only about books, because these people are assuming computers and the Web have replaced the need for libraries and, by extension, librarians. My usual answer to that question is that I believe there will always be a need for librarians because they serve as information gatekeepers. By that, I mean librarians know how to find the required information in all types of sources, considering the actual needs of the questioner, their knowledge level, their true question, the depth of their research needs, and the speed at which they must have results. As information gatekeepers and professionals, librarians must know how, where, when, why, and other options in relation to the research topic, and they must understand who is conducting the research and why they are doing so. That type of librarian will always be needed. Library users will not always have a great depth of knowledge with respect to all of the types of research sources that are available, so they may not always select the best sources for answers to their problems.

Additionally, it is not just the public services, "out front with the users" type of librarian who is needed these days. Those who acquire and organize library materials and resources are needed just as badly, especially as information on the Internet expands and the way materials are supplied changes. No one person can do or know everything.

The challenge the information gatekeeper faces is keeping up to date in all areas, and knowing the available materials well enough to think of using them. The Internet has added many helpful research resources—as well as many bad and misleading resources. It is the librarian's job to know the difference. It is also the librarian's job to know how to find other sources if the usual or previously used ones do not work for a particular patron. No one can possibly keep up with every addition to the Internet, Lexis, Westlaw, or book resources. However, research skills that are honed until they become second nature will allow the librarian to find what is needed. That includes also knowing when to seek assistance from an online service representative or reference source, or from an expert in a certain field. It is simply not conceivable to me that the world will stop needing librarians.

Our expertise should always be needed as long as we make sure we continue to be the ones to whom people still turn for answers to their questions.

An Increasing Role

Since I have been involved in academics throughout my entire career, I actually see increasing uses for our skills as the world becomes more technological. As academic law librarians, we must take this opportunity to become teachers of all types of research tools, especially technological tools. Teaching is at the fundamental core of a librarian's being. I seldom answer a reference question without trying to teach the user something. Our goal should always be to assist the user in learning how to answer the question they asked so they can find the answer themselves the next time around. Although we may not always be totally successful in that, if the user at least returns to ask us the same question again, we have achieved a partial success: it proves the user felt we were helpful the first time and that we should be helpful again. I often tell students they should always ask for help before they wind up pounding their heads against the wall in frustration. By the time they have reached that level, nothing they hear will be a learning experience. If they are that frustrated with their research or problem, they are likely also near a point of surrender, and we can only try to save the student's sanity and hope they will come to us sooner the next time.

There are multiple methods of teaching and sharing knowledge, and librarians are trained to use those methods. Teaching can be at an individual level or a classroom level. Not all of us have the same skills, so not all of us should attempt to teach at all levels. However, there is a required point of view for the academic law librarian, especially those in public services. We should always have the goal of assisting the user in *finding* an answer, not *handing* them an answer. This is not always easy to achieve—students often want the answer given to them. Doing so, however, only ensures that they will not learn how to find the answers themselves. That is certainly not the optimum use of our skills. Even if you know students do not believe they will need that information again, try to teach them how to use the materials. The methodology is often transferable, even if the question differs completely the next time.

For academic law librarians, and indeed all law librarians, adaptability is essential. Law students today are very different from law students of even five or ten years ago, let alone twenty. There are more than just generational differences, although those certainly play a role as well. Today's students are accustomed to doing multiple things at one time, although some do so better than others do. They have grown up with computers, and are used to getting immediate answers and information. They have also moved from desktop computers to laptop computers at a high rate, taking advantage of the portability to expand their continuous use of computers. They are more comfortable taking notes and exams on a computer than writing them by hand. They are also less easy to keep engaged. They do not seem to believe it is rude to carry on an in-person conversation while texting or instant messaging one or more people at the same time. They also do not seem to believe it is rude to spend class time texting, messaging, shopping, surfing, or anything else that can be done on a laptop.

Knowing the students of today can help us adapt to their needs. We must rise to the challenge of finding new ways to communicate with today's students. Many of those ways involve technology. The old saying of "If you can't beat 'em, join 'em" is true here. Librarians may use those very same means of electronic communication that their students use to talk to each other. Not only will it help you communicate with the students, but it will also put your name in front of them on a frequent basis, which should help spur business. Personally, I love it when a student stops to tell me that something I mentioned in a class or conversation led them to look at a new resource or Web site. It is not always easy to tell whether students are listening and processing what you tell them or teach them. If they are so excited by a Web page or resource that they wish to tell me how they are using it, they have learned an important lesson and will likely spend more time doing what they must do to continue to learn.

Developing New Procedures and Practices

Although it is likely a great idea, most librarians do not regularly reconsider procedures and practices that are occurring within their libraries. Library staff members usually proceed according to what they have done before, without considering what could be done differently. If questions arise, they may be discussed and shared, but usually not with a view toward possible change. Change is a frightening concept, although I believe we all change and adapt to some extent, even when we do not realize that is what we are doing. For example, effective reference librarians are much quicker now to recommend an online or electronic alternative for information than they were a few years ago. Where we may have previously used book resources first, we tend now to find an electronic resource first for many students. This is likely not a change any of us made purposefully. It is simply a response to current students' preferences and the hugely increased amount of information now available online.

New situations arise from time to time, however, which force reconsideration of a procedure or practice. Also, new people joining a library staff can result in changes being made. The trick is to make certain that changes or new procedures do not happen simply for change's sake. They should happen because they make sense, they assist in the overall goals and duties of the staff, or they make things easier in some way. They should never cause harm to existing procedures or stress out staff members with no understandable or possible benefits.

When a new staff member starts working at a library, he or she will naturally compare procedures at the new library with procedures from the library they worked at previously. That is understandable and expected. However, forcing a new procedure on a new library just because it worked at an old library is not a good idea. No two libraries are exactly alike. As staff members change within an institution, even that library will not completely be as it once was. It is frankly ignorant to believe the same procedure will work in exactly the same way at two different places. At the same time, one of the best things about bringing new people into a library is that they bring with them new experiences and expertise. However, that does not mean changes should happen immediately or quickly. A new person must get to know the staff and the policies of the new library before any consideration of change occurs, unless there happens to be some problem that truly must be addressed soon. If a change is made, it is essential that the person introducing the change be willing to reject it or refine it if it does not work. That person must also be willing to accept the opinions of the other staff members—and all staff must work to give new procedures a chance.

One of the worst things that can happen is for a new hire to believe they know more than anyone else at the library. This is seldom, if ever, true. Even if it were true with some of the staff, the new staff member will not make friends or win respect by pointing out "errors" or problems without first discovering if there are very good reasons for procedures to be what they are. Criticizing without understanding is one of the best ways to ensure staff will not want to make any changes you suggest. It also makes you look extremely foolish. Another terrible source for change is the management person who really has lost touch with the everyday functioning of the library. Changes made by this person often do not include consideration for all who will be affected. Again, change made for change's sake, and not with any actual thought of improvement in the library, will often lead to disaster and ill will.

Still, changes must be made from time to time. And, as stated above, often the best way to decide if change is needed is for someone to look at a procedure from a new point of view. Students and faculty may also be sources for changes in policies or procedures. It is essential that staff members have some investment in how they perform their jobs so they perform to a high level. Changing procedures must be seen not as a criticism of staff performance, but instead as an enhancement or improvement that will make performance easier or a process better. If a change is introduced immediately after someone had a problem, or is obviously personal to a staff member, the staff is likely to be upset with their manager and will be less supportive of the change. Involving all affected people in a discussion of changes is therefore very important. Sometimes it is difficult to include all key players from the beginning. However, throughout the development of the new procedure there will hopefully be opportunities for input from multiple people. Also, once the procedure has begun, all people affected must be allowed and encouraged to provide feedback and criticism. Dictators are seldom loved or respected. People who build teams and encourage participation are more likely to maintain a steady staff and ensure that staff members will work together happily.

New procedures may take time to develop, or may be based on ideas that are discovered in other locations or from participation in meetings and conventions. As they are developed, it is essential that consideration be given as to how they will predictably affect others. Not all effects may be predictable, but thought should be given to possible bad or good results. Using multiple people to help develop a new procedure is likely to lead to discovery of the highest number of predictable outcomes. Additional people may need to be consulted as the procedure develops, and some of those may be people outside the library's staff. As the procedure is implemented, input from all concerned must be sought. This process may involve only a few staff members, or it may include all constituencies of the law school. Concerns must be addressed, and problems should be investigated and resolved. A change that is meant to speed up efficacy of a process should do so—and hopefully in a noticeable way. Comments should be sought. Most important is that the goals or purposes of the change be stated at the beginning of the implementation. Everyone must agree to try the procedure, and everyone must also agree to support whatever end results occur. No fault should attach to a failed experiment—if it fails, it may still produce an enhancement to the old procedure or the next new try.

No one likes change. However, people often change without realizing it. All people we meet and come to know will hopefully affect our lives in some way. If a change is made in the work environment, it should be a change for the better or to make someone's job easier. It must not simply be implemented because one individual has the power to change your life, and will do so without your input or participation. Procedures that are discussed with all concerned, that include clearly stated goals, and that are implemented with the assumption that they must work or be discarded will seldom be met with unhappiness or dissension. If they are, another look is likely warranted.

A dissenter usually just wants to be heard. If reasoning and explanations for the changes follow consideration of the dissent, it should disappear. If it does not, you must then weigh the importance of the change against the strength of the dissent, and be willing to make additional changes or return to the former procedure. However, it is important to make sure you can never be accused of listening to some staff or participants and not others. If that is what you are doing, *you* will likely need to make a change—possibly to a new job. You need to make change at least palatable, considering the views and needs of all involved parties, and take the time to engage all parties in the process so they are invested in the results. You may then be able to set up regular times to re-evaluate all procedures and policies, and keep improving and expanding the functions of the library.

New Technologies and Research Tools

To understand how librarians' roles have responded to new technology, one need only look at current course offerings at library schools. There are far more technology-related courses offered now than there were not so long ago. The presumption that proceeds from that fact is that librarians need to embrace new technologies. Because of the longstanding availability of Lexis and Westlaw, law librarians are probably even more willing than other types of librarians to use electronic resources. Certainly, those systems have evolved significantly through the years to include far more information in a much more accessible and user-friendly mode. Primarily though, they encouraged legal researchers to use computer resources so long ago that their use is simply assumed today. At one time, law firms could choose not to subscribe to either system and still be effective. That is not really true any longer. The ease of availability at the law schools certainly helps to ensure that new graduates will be expecting to have access to one system at least wherever they work.

It is essential that law librarians lead the way in embracing new technologies and research tools. Academic law librarians must learn about these things, because law students will be familiar with them. If we do not keep up with the resources and technology that law students arrive knowing how to use, we will lose credibility from the beginning. Does this mean we must all be able to build computers, reformat hard drives, or add software to computers? No, it is not essential that we can handle the hardware end or any of the technology issues that are better handled by information technology professionals. However, understanding the use of equipment, knowing that new operating systems exist, and understanding what students are talking about when they describe their new electronic "toys" are all things librarians can do. I do not know everything about computers, but students sometimes ask me questions because they think I know more than I do. I then take them to our information technology people for the help they need. However, the fact that they asked me means they believe I am at least up to date on technology. I take that as a compliment, and a challenge to continue using and learning new resources—and I usually ask the information technology person what they did to resolve the student's problem so I can learn a little more.

To be successful in fulfilling a librarian's role, a librarian must learn how, or at least when, to use new technology and electronic resources, and incorporate them whenever possible. This process can take different forms. We may use various communication forms to connect with the students and inform them of things that are happening in the library. We may also use The West Education Network or Blackboard course management systems, which allow faculty to produce individual Web sites for their course materials or to hold a question-and-answer session or reference question chat. We may introduce new resources to specific classes or include them in classes we teach. We should certainly at least add them to the resources we consult in assisting students at the reference desk. We may also add resource links to our online catalogs and Web sites to encourage all of our users to try them.

Another challenge for law librarians today is the number of topics that can be described as "law and" topics. More and more students and faculty are researching subjects that should not be totally researched using only law resources. We must know about medical, humanities, scientific, and business resources, usually held or subscribed to by university or other libraries, not by law libraries. If we are lucky, the other libraries have excellent access to these resources in their Web sites. If not, and if they are nearby, we may need to refer students and faculty to those locations. Even if we have to learn how to use the resources ourselves because we may not have used them before, at least we are assisting our primary patrons in finding all aspects of the information they require. Hopefully, we have also developed a friendly relationship with librarians in these other locations so we can call on them to assist us and our patrons, knowing we will reciprocate.

Expanding the limits of our collection to include the resources available from other collections is a remarkably excellent way to add resources cheaply or for no cost to our libraries. Since so many disciplines have legal aspects, it is inevitable that students and faculty will require some non-law resources for statistics, explanations of terms, or other ways of bringing added depth to their legal research. It is also essential that we help find those additional materials, however we can do so.

Marketing the Library's Services

I—just like many of my fellow librarians—was not a business major in college. I have no interest in business topics, and math is not my friend. However, it has become clear that libraries must get involved in marketing, at least to some extent. Academic law libraries are probably some of the last sheep to come to the fold, but we can learn a great deal about marketing from our friends in law firms and other types of law libraries who have known the importance of marketing their services for many years.

Marketing and public relations topics have long been discussed at library conventions and lunch programs. I will admit I never paid that much attention to these topics in the past. I always believed students and faculty knew the value of our librarians and library, and that they would come to us whenever they needed us. However, I am now reformed. I have been surprised to learn that law students, and even some faculty, are not always aware of the services we can provide or cannot provide. Therefore, it behooves us to make certain they find out.

Academic law librarians have excellent ways available to them to communicate new services or continuing services to students and faculty. We may send out e-mail messages. We may discuss services in classroom settings as we teach, or in committee meetings with faculty. I have found that our faculty members are often some of our biggest proponents, encouraging their students to consult with the librarians on writing projects or class assignments. We should also try to schedule sufficient amounts of reference desk hours so all students have a chance to consult us when they need us. We may produce newsletters, electronically or in paper form, that highlight library services and staff members.

With new technology, we have additional and less traditional ways to market our services. We may develop regular question-and-answer chat sessions on the Web, focused on specific topics or classes, or in whichever direction they are led. We may set up a reference question-specific e-mail address that multiple librarians may access and answer, a resource that provides twenty-four-hour access for questioners—thereby giving students an opportunity to ask their questions as they think of them, no matter the time of day or night. We may develop ongoing searchable blogs to discuss questions we have been asked multiple times or how-to types of informational guides. We may also develop extensive research path-finders and guides that are available on our Web sites, internal or external, to assist users whenever they need to find certain information. All of these types of resources market our abilities and services. We should always include our names and contact information on these resources so students know us and will think of asking us questions the next time they have them.

Law students sometimes enjoy the faceless types of reference opportunities the most. They often believe they are the only ones asking what they see as stupid questions. Therefore, they appreciate the separation that comes from asking questions on the phone or through the computer. Hopefully, providing answers in this way will encourage those same students to come into the library and ask their questions in person the next time. If not, at least they have been introduced to the skills and knowledge of our librarians, and will know we can help them.

Marketing can also be done with bribes, such as gifts, prizes, or candy won for answering some questions, finding resources, or being the first to answer daily research questions. However, these things are more difficult to do at a law school than at a law firm, simply because of the larger number of clients. Law schools with 300, 400, 500, or more students cannot award only one or two prizes. Some percentage of the total student body would need to have a chance at winning, and this would add greatly to the costs involved. Therefore, prizes are not likely to be the best choice for marketing in the academic law library.

Budget Allocations

The academic law library is usually the department with the largest portion of the non-personnel budget in a law school. As a result, faculty and administrators often consider the library as the richest department. If these individuals are more aware of how libraries operate, they realize a good-sized budget is necessary to maintain a library's collection, let alone help it grow. Others, however, see a library's budget as money that could increase their salaries, pay for their travel, buy new furniture, support the moot court program, provide more barbecues and free meals, allow for more research assistant hours, or generally ease monetary restraints on any and all pet projects or unfunded dreams.

Obviously, law school budgets have increased rapidly over the years. As salaries, supplies, power, equipment, and all aspects of operation have increased, tuition charges have also increased proportionately. As the price of attending law school has risen, the need to account for each dollar and spend it wisely has also risen. Private and public school administrators must remember that most students will be paying their tuition over the three to five years of law school by getting loans and credit that will have to be repaid. It is not unusual for new graduates to begin their careers with a home mortgage-sized debt from school tuition hanging over their heads—and students are well aware of how much money they are paying. They will tell anyone how well—or not—they believe their tuition dollars are being spent.

All of these opinions and competing costs affect the size of the library's budget. Years of no budget increases (or worse, budget decreases) will also affect how far the budget goes. Publisher costs rise just as everyone else's costs rise. Librarians are often mystified as to how dramatically some prices increase within a short period, but at the same time, they expect prices to rise. Therefore, even if a library's budget for materials increases, how far that budget goes may still decrease. Consequently, academic law libraries generally have to weigh the usefulness of each subscription and purchase against the usefulness of others throughout the fiscal year.

The depth of the cuts that will be necessary may not be known at the start of the fiscal year. One reason for this is that librarians cannot possibly guess how high publisher increases will be. Also, universities sometimes must make budget cuts as the academic year progresses. Expected tuition amounts may not be met, causing the need for budget cuts later in the year. Also, changes in faculty research interests or the production of new products or electronic sites may absorb dollars that were expected to be spent in another way.

Law schools that face budget cuts at the start of their fiscal year or at any point throughout the year usually look to the library's budget for the necessary percentages. The budgets in the law school itself seldom have many portions that are not tied up with salaries or benefits, making it very difficult to find dollars that can be cut. Therefore, whether they want to or not, the deans will usually have to force some or most of the required budget cuts to come from the libraries' budgets. Librarians have sometimes battled this inevitability by spending as much of their budgets as possible at the beginning of the fiscal year, although there is some danger in doing so. We all know that our own creditors expect prompt payments every month. They do not allow us to skip a month or two just because we have already spent our money. Publishers and suppliers of library materials are no different. However, libraries sometimes do run out of money before the end of the fiscal year. That is frankly seen as preferable to having money left over at the end of the fiscal year because the librarian was cautious in spending. No department wants to give money back, nor does the law library generally want the law school to believe it can raid the library's budget as needed since that budget was not totally spent.

The overriding truth is that costs will rise whether budgets do or not. Some publishers or service providers may hold costs when they know their customers are facing bad economic times, but that charity will not continue forever. It is usually the director of the law library who has final approval of all expenses and budget issues. If the director has good relationships with publishers and providers, the library will usually be more likely to get consideration at times of difficulty. The law library will likely continue to receive the largest non-salary part of the total law school budget, especially if its budget includes technology purchases. We have long-established uses for budget dollars, particularly serial subscriptions, online services, and monographic purchases. If we have automated our acquisitions process, we can also produce multiple reports and evidence of the need for those dollars. Automation also allows us to know quickly how much money is spent, appropriated, and encumbered. These types of explanatory resources help keep library budgets where they need to be, as much as that process can be controlled.

Training the Next Generation of Law Library Managers

Specific types of managerial training cannot really be generalized in terms of their importance for the next generation of law school librarians. However, I have always believed the best managerial training for a law school librarian is on-the-job training. This is one of those areas where "apprenticeship" may also be extremely useful. It is, in my view, essential that you meet other managers in addition to your own so you have a group of people whom you may ask for advice and guidance as you navigate your career.

On-the-job training takes different forms. Unfortunately, you may sometimes witness how *not* to manage, as well as techniques to remember and emulate—and you should learn from both sides. A bad manager does not make one's life easy in the workplace, but you may learn a great deal from that person. Hopefully, even bad managers have some good skills that will be positives you may take from the relationship. Watching how specific types of situations are handled by the managers you work with or near is probably the best way to learn management techniques.

Of course, future managers should also have certain personality traits. Wanting to be a manager simply because you think you should be in charge and/or because the money is better is not the reason to follow that career path. Hopefully, job satisfaction is worth something to you. Many people find that the personnel side of library management is not their strength— and that is probably the most important aspect of good library management. Personnel management can be learned, but the heart behind it must exist. I suspect some people are happier handling personnel issues without involving their emotions or empathy. Perhaps that can work, but it is certainly not what I am used to or prefer. Management involves leadership. Leadership involves respect. Respect is earned from actions. Actions must be sincere and should always indicate that you tried your best to do what was right. If evidence of that is shown, even failure can be forgiven.

Other good traits for a manager include an ability to see the big picture as well as the smaller, an open and extroverted personality, excellent communication skills, and even better listening skills. These things may be learned, to an extent. However, once again I believe a person who has natural tendencies for these traits will do better than one who may be continually learning them. A manager should also be willing to make hard decisions and changes when necessary. A good manager knows that each person is a unique individual, and treats each person accordingly. This does not mean some people should get better treatment. It simply means some people may need to be told something in a different manner, told something more times, shown how to do something as they are told about it, or handled in some other unique way.

Working for and knowing good managers are the best ways to learn good management techniques. Good managers should also want to train or mentor others who have plans to become managers. Sometimes techniques that work for one person may not work quite the same for another. However, even if the specifics cannot be duplicated, the reason or purpose behind a management strategy should still be teachable.

It also helps to observe managers at different levels. Middle managers or unit managers have different tasks and powers than the uppermost managers. Middle managers are generally more involved in the day-to-day aspects of the library's operation and with implementing policies decided upon by upper management. A librarian who hopes to become a manager may wish to plateau at one of the lower levels. There are positives and negatives in every position. Therefore, the librarian should match those job requirements to their own skills and interests. Some people are amazing middle managers, but they cannot stand the politics or problems of the uppermost manager level. One of my managers once told me he thought the reason I had not decided whether to try for library director positions was that I understood the job all too well. At the time, I was not thrilled with his suggestion, but I have come to consider it fairly complimentary.

Knowing multiple library directors is always an excellent way to prepare for management. Directors can be asked for their opinions, which they will always give, and for anything they specifically know about a library, staff, or law school administration. I have used my contacts many times over the course of my career. Since they know me fairly well, their advice is almost always much more worthwhile and pointed for my particular needs. Even if they are unaware of the people who are involved in a certain situation, they can still give advice about the job I am seeking, the people I am trying to hire, or whatever other advice I require. These contacts may also be valuable for recommendations and nominations to fill jobs, for your library's needs or for your own advancement. Fortunately or unfortunately, the academic law librarian world is not that large. Therefore, the people who have served multiple institutions or significant years as library directors are usually the best resources you may use when applying for positions, or when deciding if you should apply.

Even though the academic world is small in some ways, it is large enough that there will be competition for the higher-level management positions. Not so very long ago, many people rose through the ranks to become library directors fairly quickly. Most of those were males, but some females were among the fast risers as well. Promotion is less likely to happen as quickly these days. With the number of middle managers looking to ascend often being higher than the number of director positions that are currently open, some managers have to wait for other positions to open.

Hopefully, while they wait, they will continue to observe and reinforce their belief that directorships are right for them. After all, many librarians do not want to take management positions. My best advice is that you should feel that being a director is something you want to do because you believe you will be able to do good things for a library. We all know the stories of library directors who took those positions for the money, and then proceeded to lay all of their work off onto their staff. These are not the directors to emulate. Find successful managers and learn from them. Then, if the job still interests you, try management—and always know in your heart if being a library director works or does not work for you and for the library.

Key Law Librarian Skills

Today's law librarians must be experts at many things. Many of the skills required are technology-based. As I have stated previously, each person is different and will have different abilities. The skills necessary for law librarians may be somewhat universal, but each individual will vary in the level of their skills. Even though academic law libraries generally have good-sized staffs, they are not usually as large as those in university libraries. Therefore, there should be a certain amount of cross-training that occurs in the academic law library. It could happen that all librarians will perform reference duties to some extent. On a given day, someone may be called upon to cover the circulation desk, open the library, or do some task that is not normally within their job duties, but which is necessary at that moment to ensure the smooth functioning of the library. Despite that possibility, each type of position would carry its own needed skill set for the librarian filling the position. Some skills cross all positions, but the depths of knowledge needed will differ. A public services librarian, for instance, does not need to know how to catalog and classify a book, but they must at least understand the process sufficiently so they know how to look for and find call numbers and what they mean.

Law librarians usually have an idea of what department they want to be in when they begin their careers. That idea may change as their interests develop, or as they discover more about the functions of various positions. Even though there is likely to be some skill set cross-over, it will seldom be as complete as would be the case with law firm librarians, or institutions with smaller staffs. In those libraries, an individual may be required to do several different tasks each day. Academic law librarians are usually primarily focused on one area, such as cataloging, acquisitions, serials, reference, access services, faculty support, or administration.

In addition to having a specific focus, librarians should try to have an idea of what their goals are in the profession. Do they wish to remain in technical or public services? Do they want to go to a library that has positions in international law or the technology side of things? Do they want to remain at the librarian level or work toward a management-level position? If management, do they look toward the director's chair, or would they be happier at the middle management level? All of these questions must be answered, and those answers will affect the skills a librarian should develop. It may take years for a person to decide what direction to take, but that will likely make them more of an expert in a certain area when a decision is finally made.

Technology skills are an absolute requirement for all law librarians today. Technical services librarians must be able to use thoroughly the various aspects of the online catalog system, and they should be familiar with using the Internet and certain software programs as needed. Public services librarians should have those same skills, except that they will likely know the intricacies of the online catalog technical systems less. They must also be able to search the Internet to answer questions and support the research needs of their primary clients—law students and faculty. They may also need to have the ability to use older technology, such as compact discs and microfiche readers. All librarians must know how to use today's printers and copiers, and even the telephone system is likely more advanced than it once was.

Reference librarians must be experts at using Westlaw, Lexis, Loislaw, and free Web resources, as well as any other Web resources to which the law library subscribes. They should also know how to find information outside of the law to support those research needs, which often involves being familiar with the resources provided by the university's library. All of these skills must be maintained, updated, and continually refreshed so the latest technology resources are present in the librarians' minds, along with all of the book titles and other materials that are physically located in the library, so students and faculty can be shown to the resources that will answer their questions most efficiently and effectively.

In addition to technology skills, law librarians must have good people skills. We deal with all types of people on a daily basis. Some of those people are lost, frustrated, angry, confused, or feeling another strong emotion. Some of those people are law faculty or administrators, law students, staff members, or people from outside of the law school entirely. We cannot deal with each of these people in each of these situations in exactly the same way. We must understand the situation quickly and try to ease the patron's frustration or anger as we lead them to an answer. We may have to instruct a member of the public on how to use a source while also ensuring that they understand the limits of how much help we may provide. We may have to tell a law faculty member, as nicely as possible, that we are not their research assistants, but would be happy to instruct whoever is in that role. I have seen librarians who are experts at handling all types of situations, and I have seen librarians who are less successful. We must be flexible and be able to read people well. We must be able to calm people, defuse difficult situations, and remove people from those difficulties as quickly as possible. These are the necessary people skills for successful problem solving.

One of the most vital skills a librarian must have is the ability to listen. We must hear what the patrons are saying—and what they are not saying. Few patrons actually ask the questions they need to ask, and few patrons believe answering their questions will often take a lengthy amount of time. Once we have listened and asked our own questions, we must then be excellent communicators in order to help the patrons understand our answers.

We must also be excellent listeners and communicators in terms of dealing with other staff members. We should always think about what we are doing and if someone else needs to know about it. Should others be consulted before we perform the task? We will all make mistakes in this area, but if we at least try to consider the impact of our actions on others, those mistakes will hopefully be limited in nature.

The greatest skill required of a law librarian is teaching. Teaching is done at all levels. We may have to teach a staff member how to do something. We may have to teach individual students how to use a resource. We may have to teach a faculty member how to use a new electronic resource or a specific aspect of a known resource. We may even have to teach an entire class or several sections of a class. Not every librarian does all of these things at the same expertise level. However, it is inevitable that all will have to do at least some teaching. After all, we are part of an academic institution. Teaching is at the most fundamental base of academics. By accepting a position with an academic institution, we are accepting that teaching will be part of our job. There should be no exception.

Just as learning from others is one of the best ways to gain managerial experience, it is best to learn the skills I have described by doing the job and by watching others do their jobs. Even though some of these skills are natural and part of your personality, they are generally also trainable to some extent. Watching others teach will hopefully make it easier when you must teach something. Understanding how a librarian eased a patron's anger should help you do the same when you are in that situation. Learning from the expertise of the people with whom you work is a big part of the reason you work with others. As a new law librarian, you must learn to ask questions and observe. Those of us who have been in the profession for a longer time may not always realize that you were unsure of how to answer a question or handle a certain situation. You must understand that learning continues after your formal education. If you accept that, you will gain the skills you need to develop into an excellent law librarian at any level you wish to attain.

Final Thoughts

I do not truly believe the role of an academic law librarian is changing. The process, the amount of information that is available, the way we impart information—all of these areas are changing. However, the fundamental purpose of an academic law librarian is and has always been to provide information to our faculty, staff, and students. The challenge is doing that efficiently, effectively, and with the best information available.

We must always be teachers. We must teach each other and our patrons. Just as teaching is the basis for an academic institution, it is the basis for an academic law library. At times, we may not even realize we are teaching. When we reinforce students' knowledge by telling them they are doing their research properly, we are teaching just as much as when we first tell them how to do a task. Many people need to hear something more than once. Some even need to hear the same thing in different ways. No matter how many times you have said the same thing in a given day, you are still teaching each person to whom you give that message. Thinking of your day in those terms can usually improve what may have seemed to be a very boring or frustrating time.

Teaching in the classroom is also important, if you are able to do that. Classroom teaching gives the law librarian exposure to the students that we do not otherwise get. Helping students on an individual or even small group level in the library is expected of a librarian. However, students who see librarians in a classroom setting are often more likely to seek them out whenever they have questions. We are equated, at least to some extent, with their other professors. That is extremely beneficial to the impression students have of librarians.

One of the most important things librarians can do is to continue learning themselves. To do that, we must accept that there is always something we can learn. Part of learning is listening as well. If we are not getting our point across to our students, it may be because we did not hear their questions completely. Maybe we cut them off, thinking we knew what they were going to say. We have all had those confused conversations where one person is trying to ask one question, and the other person is actually answering another. Hopefully, at some point, the confusion is discovered, because otherwise the student will leave more confused and less trusting of our abilities. Law students can often help us change our own way of thinking, although we still bring our knowledge and skills to the table. Certainly, this entire book is about how law students have changed over the years—and if we do not change our way of dealing with them, we will not be doing our jobs properly. We must continue to learn from them, from each other, and from every transaction we have.

Without the ability to continue to learn, librarians will be left behind. If we want our profession to continue to thrive, we must grow as information specialists. Where the information comes from should be nearly irrelevant. That can differ widely, depending on the person requiring the information and how much information they truly need. Getting the students, faculty, and staff to the information they require is the primary goal of a law school librarian. If we are unable to serve our clients because of our own lack of knowledge or our unwillingness to learn, we will fail them, and we will very likely not get a second or third chance to try again. Learning as you teach someone else is perfectly acceptable. Learning because you gave incorrect information and checked it afterwards is a mistake.

The academic law librarian world is relatively small. We are fortunate in that it is also fairly mobile. Chances are we will meet many people in our field—at conventions, during interviews, or simply in going to work every day. If we see every meeting as a possible learning experience, we will inevitably become better at what we do. Attending conventions and local programs are keys to our growth as individuals and as a profession. Sharing what we know with others and altering what we do because of an idea someone gave us should be the most satisfying parts of our jobs. We must be the ones who change, more than our roles do. If we adapt to the changing world, our changing patrons, and our changing tasks, we will continue to learn, to grow, and to keep our profession sharp and fresh. Those should also be aspects of our job. Stagnation is death for a good reason. Change may be difficult to take sometimes, but it is part of life. It should also be part of our profession as academic law librarians.

Nancy L. Strohmeyer is currently the associate director and head of public services at the Barry University School of Law Library. She has also worked at the Loyola University New Orleans School of Law and the University of Arkansas at Fayetteville School of Law.

Ms. Strohmeyer's own education was in Illinois, with a B.A. and M.L.S. from the University of Illinois-Urbana-Champaign and a J.D. from Southern Illinois University. She has worked with the American Association of Law Libraries placement committee for several years.

Acknowledgement: *I want to express my gratitude to all my family, friends, acquaintances, and people who passed through my life in any way for helping me become the person and professional I am. I also thank Kim Wolenberg, my Westlaw representative, for suggesting me as someone to write for this book. Kim, it was fun, so I owe you a lunch!*

Adapting to New Technologies and Managerial Demands

Roy M. Mersky

*Harry M. Reasoner Regents Chair in Law
and Director of Research*

University of Texas at Austin School of Law,

Jamail Center for Legal Research,

Tarlton Law Library

Originally, the faculty was responsible for managing the law school library. However, at some point law schools hired clerical persons and other professionals to perform that function. By the 1950s, several people with both law and library degrees became interested in law librarianship, and they were much sought after by law schools. As time went by, having both a law degree and a library degree became almost a requirement for a director's position, and today most law school library directors have such degrees. Most library directors also have faculty status, although there has recently been a reluctance to give faculty status to new directors, and this issue has become a controversial subject.

The culture of the legal academy seems to have changed since the 1970s, in that professionals with working knowledge of the substantive law and of legal research methods have come to be seen as not quite as academically prestigious as philosophers and sociologists of legal theory. Thus, law librarians (who are research specialists) and legal clinicians (who have practical legal expertise) have grown less likely to hold tenured faculty positions. Tenured faculty, on the other hand, are judged and evaluated less on their provision of expertise to the public, the legal profession, the practicing bar, and its various professional organizations and associations. Rather, publication of theoretical articles in scholarly journals is seen as more important and desirable. The difficulty in finding well-qualified and well-trained law librarians, which I mention below, is also relevant here. There are not very many candidates for law librarian jobs who have the experience and the unique combination of skills necessary to excel right away. Few with the necessary librarianship expertise and experience have published as many scholarly articles as other faculty. Thus, many law librarians do not have the level of intellectual confidence from their deans that would be required to see tenure more frequently granted to them.

Meanwhile, in some ways, the role of the law library director remains unchanged. A law library director disseminates information, collects books, and makes them accessible with various classifications, and it is our job to tell the faculty and the students what resources the library has through various marketing efforts. However, the skills that are needed to manage a law school library are much more sophisticated these days than only a few years ago. For example, a library director must be very knowledgeable with respect to constant advances in technology. He or she must understand online digitization and databases—there are no more printed encyclopedias these days, as they are all online. Not only must the library director have the ability to find this information, but he or she must also be able to interpret it and pass it on to the users of the library.

Key Services of a Law School Library

Teaching the legal research aspects of law is the primary responsibility of a law school library. Indeed, to practice law successfully, students must know how to find accurate statutes, case law, and decisions. Such research skills are necessary to assist the clients that today's law students will be working for in the future.

To help our students meet the challenges of using new library technology, we offer a number of special classes in research skills. We work with the students both one on one and in the classrooms. Perhaps our greatest challenge in this endeavor is keeping up with the rapid pace of new developments in technology, and getting the financial funding to support its implementation.

Essential Skills for Today's Library Director

Looking to the future, we need more middle managers for our law libraries. Many people with law and library degrees have no real experience or training for administration or management careers. There is a big gap in that area. For example, few job candidates have significant practical experience in establishing budgets, monitoring budget performance, generating financial reports, and finding and implementing cost and scale efficiencies, yet these skills are valuable in connection with virtually every aspect of library management, from acquisitions to inventory to marketing to publication and sales. Also, law librarians must wear an increasingly complex array of hats, from educator to research director to planner of expansions to the physical plant, book collections, or digital resources. This is superimposed on the variety of fundamental management tasks already mentioned.

Another reason the next generation of law school librarians and directors must be knowledgeable in the area of technology is so they can deal with vendors more effectively. In the past, we may have bought a book for $25, whereas now we are spending between $1,000 and $100,000 for online materials and technology. While many of our students use traditional online research tools such as Google, we need to be familiar with all of the technologies that result in acceptable legal research.

Marketing Strategies and Budget Considerations

It is essential for a law school library to implement effective strategies for communicating its services to its students and faculty members. Otherwise, they might miss valuable opportunities to enrich either their educational experience or their scholarly work. Our library, for example, publishes a regular newsletter to promote our services. We also publish an annual report that profiles the law library for our parent institution, our alumni, and our professional colleagues. It is important to demonstrate to all those connected with the library that it merits continued financial and institutional support, and the annual report, when placed in the proper hands, helps us achieve this goal. We also have a Web page, we send out e-mails, and we communicate with students and faculty in the classroom. We seek to constantly inform students, faculty, and the university community at large of the archives, traveling exhibits, special presentations, and other research materials and programs that might be relevant to their work or else of general interest. For example, if you were a medieval legal historian on the faculty here, you would probably be very disappointed if we arranged to temporarily house and display a first edition of Blackstone's *Commentaries* but you were never made aware of this fact. Similarly, students are also entitled to have access to valuable archival and human resources to aid them in their studies and future careers.

Marketing the library's services is especially important because library budgets have not grown in recent years, in most instances. Therefore, if you need to spend $100,000 for new technology resources, you may need to create fundraising events or solicit private funding.

Navigating the Changing Role of Librarianship

Today's law school librarian and/or director needs to have more experience in business administration and computer sciences, and he or she must work to develop administrative and personnel skills, as well as the skills that are necessary to be an effective teacher. Fortunately, some librarians are taking proactive steps in that direction, although a few have not caught up as of yet. However, I believe it is just a matter of time before most librarians adapt to this changing role.

It is often most difficult for librarians to gain the necessary administrative and management skills, and to understand the business aspects of this job, largely because there is no formal education and training in those areas. My recommendation is that if you have a law degree and you work in a law library, you should get some hands-on experience in terms of management, and take courses in computer science. For a law school library director to be successful, he or she must focus on self-education and training, which often includes finding a proper mentor and working with other institutions that have been successful. Becoming active in one or more professional organizations for lawyers, legal academics, librarians, or law librarians is a good way to network and find appropriate mentors.

Strong computer skills are highly important, because many legal publications are now exclusively available online, and we have to teach our students and faculty how to access and use materials that are no longer being published in print from. Research methodologies are very different these days. No longer can you simply go to a book, check an index, or look at the table of contents to find the information you need. You need to be able to access the information that is available online, and in many cases, there are certain licensing requirements and passwords that must be used in that process, which make it rather complicated.

Certain outside resources have proven instrumental in successfully managing the changing role of a law library director. For example, there is a company called Innovative Services that has helped us take control of some of the technological aspects that are required in a library.

Final Thoughts

Among the biggest challenges library directors face going forward are the many additional costs that are associated with acquiring the same information in multiple formats. Curriculums in law schools are becoming more interdisciplinary, and include many new subject areas. For example, the emphasis throughout the legal profession and the broader economy on globalization and international perspectives drives research to be more interdisciplinary in a global and cultural sense. Meanwhile, as law practice changes from the old private practice model to a new interdisciplinary paradigm that deals with an ever more complex web of business relationships and industry-specific regulations and issues, lawyers are needed who can be expert not only in the law, but also in that which it seeks to control or regulate. Thus, natural resources lawyers need access to environmental information, patent lawyers need access to engineering studies, securities lawyers need access to business and banking information, and so on. However, few libraries have seen a budget increase in terms of their allocation for information resources. In our case, the percentage of the law school budget that is allocated for new information resources has stayed at 5 percent. Therefore, one of my biggest challenges as director is to oversee the budget successfully while trying to get increased financial support for our changing needs.

For more than forty years at the University of Texas, Professor Roy M. Mersky oversaw the evolution of the school's law library into one of the pre-eminent research facilities in the nation, as well as the training of its professional library staff many of whom became law library directors around the country. In addition, he wrote extensively in the areas of legal research and Supreme Court history.

Professor Mersky was a member of the American Law Institute and a fellow of the American Bar Foundation, the Texas Bar Foundation, and the American College of Law Practice and Management. He earned his B.S. (1948), J.D. (1952), and M.A.L.S. (1953) from the University of Wisconsin at Madison.

In grateful memory of Professor Roy M. Mersky (1925 – 2008). This chapter was one of the last among many contributions Professor Mersky made to the legal and library profession.

The Librarian as Educator: Teaching Essential Research Skills

Joan Shear

Legal Information Librarian and Lecturer in Law

Boston College Law Library

From Book Finders to Information Guides

Law librarians used to be keepers of books—people who ordered books, shelved books, and found books for people. In large academic law libraries, legal reference librarians were especially needed to help people find books because the Library of Congress took such a long time to develop its law schedules that many law libraries developed their own classification systems—but without unique call numbers. When I started working at Harvard Law Library, there were still ranges of books that all had the same call number, and I heard stories of how not that long ago most of the 1.5 million books in its collection were shelved by main entry order. When I moved to Boston College Law Library a few years later, I asked my new boss how our loose-leaf services, which were not yet classified, were shelved. She was only partially joking when she replied, "Isn't it obvious? By color, of course!" What she was saying was they were shelved by publisher, and each publisher's volumes were a different color.

Today fewer people are looking for books to solve their information needs, but that doesn't mean they no longer have such needs. They are just looking in a different place: the Internet. One of my colleagues, Mark Sullivan, likes to say that the existence of the Internet guarantees continued employment for librarians. I'm inclined to agree with him, because while there is now an enormous amount of information available online, it is not always easy to find what you are looking for. The most frequently asked question at an academic law library reference desk used to be, "How do I find a case when all I know is the name?" Now that LexisNexis and Westlaw have made that question obsolete, the number-one question seems to be, "Why can't I find this older law review article on LexisNexis or Westlaw?" So for the modern law librarian, instead of being relied on for our knowledge of where to find books and what might be in them, we are called on more as experts in information and search strategies to help people find information online. In a sense, we are changing the way we do things, but not the what. We are still bringing researchers and information together.

Current Trends in Academic Librarianship

One reason why it is often not easy to find what you're looking for online is that many online sources were designed to be analogs of their print antecedents. This made for a smooth transition for those of us who learned legal research using those books, but without that context, online sources can seem poorly organized and merely quirky to today's students. That's why other academic law librarians and I are greatly concerned by the wholesale dumping of our print collections. While I agree that we can no longer maintain multiple copies of print subscriptions—nor do we need to—I do believe we need to keep "teaching sets" we can use to help illustrate the structure of the information students will eventually be using online. To become the best researchers they can be, our students need to understand that while some of our online sources actually derive useful traits from their print beginnings, others have merely inherited a bad template from their print antecedents.

Furthermore, human indexing and digesting of statutes and cases provides more efficient access to primary law, and students who have never seen these sources in print may not fully grasp the research advantage they provide.

In addition, the huge explosion in legal publishing, as well as the creation of an enormous variety of online research sources, has increased the need for librarian-educators. While law students are no doubt smart enough to figure out over time how to research things for themselves, they do not have that much time. Today's law firms can no longer afford to hire young law school graduates and then spend years giving them the practical training to be effective lawyers. They want people who can produce from day one. Even if that were not the case, junior lawyers are typically the head researchers, so the better they are trained to do research, the more valuable they will be to their employers. When I went to law school, there was only one general legal periodical index, and if you needed to find a law review article on a particular topic, you needed to use it. Now, besides there being competing general legal periodical indices employing differing theories of indexing, they are each searchable through their own native interfaces as well as through LexisNexis and Westlaw, and they are also in direct competition with full-text search databases. Simply put, there is more information available these days and more ways to look for it, and law students need someone to help them navigate the waters.

One way this has manifested itself is through increased classroom teaching, especially in the area of specialized research. As the practice of law becomes more specialized, the need for specialized research tools has increased as well. Here at Boston College, for example, we offer a variety of upper-level topical research courses in addition to a general course in advanced legal research. As far back as twenty years ago, a former student told me he wished I had introduced him to the *Standard Federal Tax Reporter* while he was still in law school where he was specializing in taxation. In those days, we had one-size-fits-all research instruction. Now that we offer a variety of specialized research classes, students in my intellectual property research class who work in boutique intellectual property law firms are glad to be trained in the use of BNA's *U.S. Patents Quarterly* online, since some of their firms do not subscribe to LexisNexis or Westlaw. While there are many research skills every lawyer needs, there are also a variety of research tools not everyone needs, but that are of enormous value to a select group of practitioners. As the practice of law itself becomes more specialized, law school librarians will need to teach more subject-specific research tools.

The Role of New—and Old—Technologies in the Research Process

In law, finding "good information" is not good enough. You must find the best information, and all the information you need. Law librarians understand the value of technology and adopted it early, but we have to make it clear to our students that technology alone is not going to solve all of their research problems. Students need to learn how to use any form of research technology to their advantage. To achieve this, we have to help our law students change their attitudes about research and gain an appreciation for the quality of information wherever found, and for the economies of effective and efficient research. That process includes reading and following directions, and then evaluating what you have found.

Despite having had a lifelong exposure to electronic information, most of today's students come into law school needing judgment about how to best use technology in legal research. For example, they are not facile with concepts such as outlining or how to use tables of contents. Many do not even realize there is such a thing as an index or catalog that can help quickly identify relevant contents in a larger work. Studies show that in most instances people who search indexed information find what they are looking for faster than those using free text searching methods. Yet because most students are so used to searching using Google, they default to full text searching, even when an available index will probably serve them better.

Another problem with keyword searches is that the search engines on LexisNexis and Westlaw can't tell the difference between the various unrelated meanings associated with a particular word. They can only locate instances of particular words, and don't always capture the context. Looking for a law review article on a particular subject, I once produced a search that only got me law review articles with footnotes that explicitly stated they weren't going to be addressing that issue in the article. A subject heading tells you what a book is really about, not just what words are chosen for a catchy title. For instance, a book with the title "Cafeteria Plans" might easily be mistaken as a book about restaurants or lunchrooms. (Cafeteria plans are actually a type of employee benefit plan, and don't have anything to do with eating.) There are some who say we should abandon our catalogs, or at least not bother with the expense of adding subject headings to catalogs when fewer people use them. In my opinion, while it may be true that an expert who already possesses the familiarity with the literature in a particular field may not benefit from subject headings, anyone who is new to that field or is crossing disciplines will get better results by using catalog subject headings—once they find the right one.

And the modern online catalog can provide context-sensitive links to full text article and other resources just as easily as it provides information about where a physical copy of a book or journal is kept in the library. This provides superior access to the "invisible Web" than a plain Web search can, and it provides access to materials available only by subscription, even when the researcher is off campus. This blending of the old-fashioned catalog with modern linking technologies provides superior access to researchers, but only if they are taught to check the catalog for resources.

Conveying Key Skills: Assisting Students in the Research Process

When my students are first exposed to what is really entailed in the research process—and the fact that there is so much information out there that they have to locate and analyze—they often feel the process is overwhelming. I have to work to instill in them the confidence that they will be able to deal with whatever research challenges come their way—skills that will ultimately help them become good lawyers. By the end of their final exam, my students are often surprised by how much they know, because they know any research problem can be solved, especially if you have a good grasp of research basics.

I use most of the standard teaching technologies in the course of teaching the research process. My classroom "lectures" are accompanied by PowerPoint slides—some with words, but more often with pictures of the insides and outsides of books as well as computer screen captures. I post all my PowerPoint shows and accompanying notes on the class Web pages using the course management system to which our university subscribes. Because I'm teaching research, students need computers and Internet connections in class, which they use to answer research challenges every ten to fifteen minutes that enable them to apply the research tool or strategy just presented. They also get follow-up research exercises to do outside of class to make sure they can apply the skills introduced in class. Assignments are collected through the course management software. Students are sometimes asked to post opinions and reviews of various research sources on threaded discussion lists. I also post answer keys with extensive feedback on any difficulties the students encountered in completing their exercises.

The most important service I can provide my students is teaching them the skills they will need to be lifelong learners as they practice law. We start with basic research skills, just as you would learn to read simple stories before you are ready to read Shakespeare—once you know the basics, you can take those skills and use them in any situation.

Years ago, I created a "learning exercise" I still like to use to help students focus more on their own learning processes. Each student is given a small stack of five pieces of colored paper. Students are asked to put down their pencils and just listen as I read them a list of numbers. As soon as I finish, they are instructed to write down on the first piece of colored paper as many of the numbers as they can remember. On the second piece of colored paper, the students are allowed to take notes as I read the same numbers aloud a second time. The third piece of paper again tests their memory of what was read to them. On the fourth piece of paper, they are allowed to look at their notes to help them remember the numbers to write. At the fifth piece of colored paper, they are asked, "What is the next number in the series?" Usually no one actually knows the number, because the numbers had seemed like random numbers, but students are encouraged to make their best guess anyway. Students are asked to compare their first and third sheets of paper. Usually a third to a quarter of the class will have more numbers correct on their first sheet and the rest will have more correct on their third sheet. Some people got more numbers correct when they were just listening because it forced them to pay more attention. Some did better when they were taking notes, because they only remember what they were able to write down, but for others the improved score was a result of having heard the numbers a second time. For some people, taking notes is an essential part of the learning process, whereas for others it can be a distraction. This part of the exercise tries to get students to focus on the fact that they shouldn't be concerned about what others do, but they need to concentrate on their own learning style to get what they need out of class. I provide notes for those for whom note-taking would be a distraction, but for those who need to take their own notes, they should use mine as a back-up.

As expected, everyone gets everything correct on the fourth page, where they consulted their notes. This helps remind the class that the notes and PowerPoint shows can enhance their learning, but only if they use them. The fifth piece of paper is used to illustrate that being able to remember something is not the same as actually understanding it. Usually a few people have managed to guess the last number in the sequence for reasons that have nothing to do with why it is the correct number. Once I explain to my students the series of numbers I read, all students can quickly figure out any number in the sequence. Understanding is vastly superior to memorizing as a way of learning, since with understanding information can be reconstructed or found again anytime it is needed.

I try to give my students lots of feedback on their assignments, especially positive feedback, since there is generally so little of that in law school. When my students have wrong answers on their assignments, I can usually see where they went astray in their approach to the research problem. But if they merely guess the right answer, I have no way of knowing that—only they know if they do not really understand something. Therefore, if they do not understand something, they need to ask for help. Students who are doing poorly will continue to do poorly if they do not ask for help, while those who ask for help and let me work with them will eventually succeed. You cannot force students to learn, but you can give them every opportunity to do so. I am responsible for teaching—the student is responsible for learning.

Determining Reliability of Information

It is more important for today's legal researcher to be critical in terms of both the content and the source of their information than researchers in the past. With the explosion of electronic publishing, it is no longer sufficient to just find legal information. It is also important to make sure the information found can be relied on. The ease and relative inexpensiveness of electronic publishing has largely removed book publishers from their role as gatekeepers and shifted much of the burden of validating information to the end user. Some states have actually discontinued their print administrative registers and substituted a cheaper but more easily accessible online version without taking any safeguards to ensure the authenticity of the electronic original.

Law students have always needed to understand that there is a difference between information that is in the form of law and is therefore binding, and other information, such as legislative history, which is simply persuasive. Now they also need to be taught to check not just who is publishing information electronically, not just to look for biases, but also to look for procedural safeguards such as digital signatures to guarantee that the information is unaltered and uncorrupted.

It is also important to teach students to write better searches so they do not have to wind up looking through so much irrelevant material. New rules allowing citations to unreported judicial decisions have only increased the need for efficient searching. In Boolean searching, there is a natural tension between precision and accuracy. Accuracy means to capture all of the relevant material, and precision means to minimize the irrelevant material. However, it is very difficult to write a perfect search that has both total precision and total accuracy. To ensure total accuracy, the researcher must examine a lot of extra and ultimately irrelevant material—and time is money. Therefore, in many cases a researcher may have to accept imperfection, since by striving to make a search more precise, it is inevitable that you may lose some good hits. So the researcher needs to be able to rely on some other means of finding that information.

Indeed, our catch phrase in this area is that we do not call the information-gathering process "one search"—we call it "research," in that if you have not approached a problem from at least two angles, you have probably missed something. By approaching a research project from at least two different angles, you minimize the possibility of missing something important. A humorous story I think illustrates this point was actually a fictional article in an April 1 issue of the *Harvard Law Record*, the law student newspaper. The article was framed by a picture of Professor Laurence Tribe facing right and an identical picture with him facing left. It purported to be about a case where he had actually argued against himself at the U.S. Supreme Court. In the article, he was asked when he first realized he was arguing both sides of the same case, to which he replied that he hadn't actually noticed that until he sat down from his first argument and then rose again to face the same court in the same case. The article went on to explain how the plaintiffs and defendants had each characterized their positions so differently, one explaining it as a separation of powers problem, while the other characterized the issue as being about the right of free speech, both topics he is passionate about, that he never really noticed they were the same case.

Key Skills for Academic Librarians

There's an old adage that says, "The more things change, the more they stay the same." I believe the true value of a law library is not as much in the books as in the librarians. Now that much information is in electronic form, it is even more important for librarians to be people who can connect researchers with the information they seek.

Years ago, I was asked what it takes to be a great academic reference librarian. I replied that you need to be clairvoyant and omniscient, which was a flip way of saying you essentially need to know what people really need no matter what question they actually ask, and be able to answer any question that comes to you. Of course, those of us who are neither clairvoyant nor omniscient must substitute a reference interview to find out what people really need and then look up that information in the most efficient way possible to make up for our limited personal knowledge.

This need is even truer in the Information Age. A computer only answers the question presented to it. It has trouble recognizing when it's being led astray. Law librarians may not (yet) be clairvoyant and omniscient, but we can come closer than even today's powerful computers. Many times, I find answers that students and faculty can't, even though we both look in the same place, because I phrase the question differently. I remember how amazed I was the very first time I was able to find a bit of tax law information for a tax professor. His superior knowledge of the subject matter didn't help him find the information he needed without the assistance of my familiarity with the organization of information.

That's why I believe good communication skills are the number-one requirement for an academic librarian. No matter where you work in an academic law library, you need to communicate with faculty, students, vendors, law school administrators, and colleagues. Teaching is a special kind of communicating that requires a collection of skills. You need to be able to present information in a way that makes it easy to understand yet complex enough to engage the student in a way that helps the student remember the information itself, the context in which it is important, and how to apply it when the time comes that the information needs to be used. You need to be able to listen to your students to find out whether the information you are trying to convey is in fact being received, and adjust your delivery method to make the information more available to students having difficulties. And you need to be able to provide your students with meaningful feedback so they can correct any misperceptions they have accidentally come away with, and so they can use it to adjust their learning strategies so they can get everything they can out of your teaching.

A good law library director is one who is able to find and retain quality staff members. The best way to do that is to make your employees happy and eager to work by empowering them to do the jobs you hired them to do. Good library directors indicate the direction they want things to move in, and then they let their people do their jobs in ways that work best for them, because everyone works best differently—we all have different strengths and weaknesses. At the same time, librarians must also be people who can work together as a team, because you need teamwork to run a library properly. One person cannot know everything, nor do everything on their own. What we create together is exponentially better than what we can create alone.

Challenges for Law School Librarians

The change from print to online sources has proven to be a mixed blessing for law school librarians. The pitfalls inherent in the technology affect both the use of the sources and the teaching of legal resources. Perhaps the biggest challenge facing today's law school librarians pertains to the fact that many incoming students think they know how to research—but they do not know how to research in this profession. Unfortunately, it is usually the people who have the most confidence in their research abilities who do not know very much about research and are doing it poorly.

Another major concern is the fact that we often have only temporary access to much of our electronic information rather than permanent, guaranteed access. Database vendors sometimes lose contracts to include information in their law school subscription packages, and we are forced to do without publications we recently had access to. As we move away from print to online resources only in an attempt to save money, we need to make sure we are not creating problems for future researchers. A number of states have already stopped publishing their official administrative codes in print. They are only published online, and therefore there is no certainty as to whether that information will always be available. Online information is often provided without any authentication, and it is important to be sure the Web site you are on has a digital signature or some other means of letting you know that what you are looking at is the real thing, and not some adulterated copy.

One of the most difficult challenges academic librarians face is making sure the people we work for—the law school administration—understand how important our work is and how many resources are involved. We do not want administrators to think, "Now that everything is electronic, we do not need librarians." Rather, we want them to say, "Now that everything is electronic, we need even more librarians." At the same time, we have to make sure the budgets for electronic resources and staffing goes up every year—and this is perhaps the toughest challenge, because it is the most important and we have the least control over it. It is also important to remind the administration that an academic endeavor such as a law school library is not an economic endeavor, and while a company is measured by the profit it makes, a school should be measured by the education it provides to its students, not how much money it saves if that short-circuits the students' education.

Overcoming Difficulties: Helpful Resources

The most helpful resource I use in overcoming any difficulties is other librarians. I consult with my colleagues regularly for assistance and advice. I consult with my co-workers daily. We will chat about the best ways to develop new programs or how to answer a particular reference question. I consult with librarians in other types of libraries in preparing classes, because I am trying to prepare my students for the world these colleagues work in. Since I am not working at a law firm or government office, I need to talk to people in those areas who can tell me how the practice of law is changing and what ramifications those changes have on my students. I also talk to law practitioners in the fields I teach specialty research courses in so I can know what is important to them as lawyers, what they are dealing with on a daily basis, and what I can do that will give my students an edge when they enter the workplace. I also try to get all the training I can, because there are always new technologies to learn and new information sources to learn about, and I attend professional meetings to hear from outside experts who keep me informed with respect to what is going on in the field.

Changing Government Regulations and Enforcement Practices

Learning law, and even more, learning legal research, is all about learning to live with change. It is not as important for law students to know what the law is today as to be able to find out what it is at the present time or at a particular time in the past, or how it is changing and how they can make the best predictions about the direction in which it is going to change.

Legal research is changing even faster than the law itself, with new research tools being introduced all the time. Every time I teach students how to update their KeyCite results, I am reminded that I was there the day West introduced this new research tool. Every year I need to update almost all of my PowerPoint slides to reflect the new interfaces on LexisNexis and Westlaw.

A few years ago, a judge found an attorney guilty of malpractice for not properly predicting that a cause of action for their client's case would exist in the future. The judge said the attorney should have been reading *Law Week* and should have known a case was in front of the Supreme Court that would soon make such a cause of action possible. In essence, the judge believed the attorney should have included in his original pleadings a cause of action that did not exist at the time he wrote the pleadings, because it would very likely be possible in the near future, after the close of the statute of limitations for bringing that cause of action. Since the attorney did not preserve his client's rights by pleading that cause of action, he was found negligent.

Although the appeals court found that the attorney could not be held responsible for not knowing about a law that did not yet exist, I believe attorneys should always strive to give their clients advice that is based not just on what the law is today, but also on where it is moving, so they can protect their clients from whatever may happen down the road. Being a lawyer is not just about being a litigator, but also an adviser. Things are constantly changing in this field, and if you are prepared to deal with constant change, you will be a successful lawyer.

Final Thoughts

As an academic librarian, it is important to always keep your goals in mind and always have a vision, because there is so much change going on and so many exciting technologies are constantly emerging that we are often tempted to try them all. However, we should always make technology the tool of what we want to accomplish—we should only use a new technology if it helps us do what we want to do.

Indeed, technology has become a hindrance to our profession in many ways, because we sometimes become so wrapped up in technology that we forget our goals. Therefore, you should never forget what you are trying to do. You need to make sure everything you do works toward fulfilling your personal goals and the mission of your employer. Simply put, everything I do should be aimed at helping Boston College Law School fulfill its mission with respect to enhancing the education of its students, the scholarship of its faculty, and its reputation in the world, and I need to find the right tools and make use of my own strengths in order to do that job in the best way possible.

Joan Shear obtained her bachelors' degree from the University of Minnesota College of Liberal Arts, her law degree from Harvard Law School, and her library degree from the Catholic University of America. While in library school, she did a reference practicum at the Law Library of Congress. After obtaining her library degree, she became a reference librarian at the Harvard Law Library. She joined the reference department at the Boston College Law Library in 1986.

Ms. Shear developed and teaches in the introduction to legal research course for the Law Librarians of New England, and the basic legal reference workshop for the American Association of Law Libraries. For many years, she co-taught in the first-year legal reasoning research and writing course. Currently she teaches advanced legal research, environmental legal research, and intellectual property research at Boston College Law School. She is developing a course on professional responsibility research for next year.

Acknowledgment: *To my husband, Matt, for his editing and encouragement.*

The Greatest Challenges
for Today's
Law School Librarians

Christopher L. Steadham, JD, MLIM

Faculty Services and Research Librarian

University of Kansas School of Law,

Wheat Law Library

The fundamental challenge facing law school librarians today is an ongoing struggle for definition and identity. Academic law librarianship is a subset of law librarianship, itself a unique hybrid of librarianship and law. By most metrics, it is a highly specialized profession.[1] Yet a remarkable amount of variation exists among law school librarians and their daily work. Rapidly evolving technologies, academic hierarchies, varied educational backgrounds, eclectic expertise, and responsibilities—all these factors contribute to a remarkably heterogonous group of professionals. This diversity is both necessary and desirable. However, such complexity can be puzzling to the uninitiated. Indeed, librarians in general have long lamented the misunderstandings that plague their public relations. As Richard A. Danner noted in his seminal article, "Redefining a Profession," "It has always been difficult for library users to understand precisely what librarians do, or why some of the people employed in libraries pointedly identify themselves as professional workers, while the work of other library employees is not considered to be professional."[2] Such problems of perception are the root of many challenges facing law school librarians in the Information Age.

Several factors contribute to this professional identity crisis. First is the paradoxical nature of specializing in something as broad as "information." Librarians are the ultimate generalists, studying the process of information transfer more than the substantive information itself. The recent buzz word "information professional" encapsulates this generalist orientation. Non-librarians, however, might understandably view this phrase with some skepticism. Strictly speaking, the term "information" encompasses enough to make every profession an "information profession." True, law librarians are more narrowly defined as "legal information professionals," but the problem persists. Most disciplines consider information on a need-to-know basis—using information as a means to an end. In contrast, to librarians, information is an end in itself. This is the distinguishing feature that gives meaning to the term "information professional." Finding more effective

---

[1] For example, the American Association of Law Libraries has approximately 5,000 individual members, a relatively small number in comparison to many professions. See www.aallnet.org/about.

[2] Richard A. Danner, "Redefining a Profession," 90 *Law Library Journal* 315, 315 (Summer 1998).

ways to communicate this crucial distinction is one of the most pressing challenges currently confronting librarians.

Whatever its drawbacks, the new emphasis on terms such as "information professional" does help to alleviate the second pertinent factor: the dreaded "L" word. The title "librarian" evokes visceral stereotypes in popular culture, many of which are quite negative in many respects. However removed from reality these prejudices may be, perceptions still matter. Law librarians are even more attuned to matters of status, connected as they are to the prestigious legal profession. It is here that academic law librarianship must lead the way in emphasizing the important connection between law librarianship and legal research. As the foremost experts in the field of legal research, law librarians possess considerable leverage in the Darwinian struggle of professions. Persuading the greater population that law librarians are crucial links in the chain of legal information, rather than clichéd caricatures, is yet another challenge facing academic law librarianship in the twenty-first century.

The third, and perhaps most potent, factor in law librarianship's struggle for definition is the perception that technology is gradually constricting the life out of the profession, and will ultimately replace librarians with electronic equivalents. Prior to the advent of electronic information technologies, librarians were the undisputed caretakers of the knowledge contained in print resources. The digital revolution has shaken the foundation of this paradigm. With databases and search engines, the thinking goes, the need for librarians has greatly diminished. What proponents of this erroneous notion fail to appreciate is the necessity of "mediation," which refers to the context information professionals can provide when navigating the vast universe of electronic information. The seemingly geometric expansion of available information has, in reality, increased the need for professionals who study the way information is structured and the pathways it follows in modern society. The expertise law librarians offer in this environment is undeniably necessary, and profitable. Young associates in law firms across the nation can attest to this fact.

The preceding discussion demonstrates that, like most professions, law librarianship entails a wide variety of components that range from mundane tasks to abstract theory. Unfortunately, popular conceptions tend to emphasize the routine and technical, while neglecting the intellectual and academic elements. Failure to appreciate the full spectrum of contributions made by librarians is what allows pessimistic views of the profession's future prospects to flourish. Those who view librarianship in more vocational, rather than professional, terms have proclaimed that "librarians will have an increasingly difficult time justifying themselves, their staffs, and their physical space to their deans and university presidents, especially now that so many academic institutions are putting so much emphasis on the bottom line."[3] While there is a grain of truth in this belief, it does not account for the ability of librarianship to evolve with changing technologies and paradigms over the years. Furthermore, with specific reference to academic law librarianship, such beliefs are typically based upon three faulty assumptions: "that only a small fraction of law ·faculty engage in research…that librarians will not add value to the research enterprise because individuals will do everything for themselves using technology, and…[the] implicit perception that the law library is unrelated to the teaching program."[4] When these false premises are corrected, the continuing vitality of academic law librarianship becomes clear. Again, the problem is one of perceptions that do not accurately reflect reality.

Clearly, the reports of librarianship's demise have been greatly exaggerated. This is especially true for academic law librarianship, a profession with several unique qualities that ensure its continuing vitality. It is, at the micro-level, a crucial component of legal education and, at the macro-level, an essential ingredient for representative democracy. Just ask any law school librarian, and they will tell you so. This central tenet of faith is ingrained within the professional culture to such a remarkable degree that there is a tendency to assume its obviousness. The problem is that few outside the profession have read the preamble to the ethical principles of the American Association of Law Libraries, stating that, "When individuals have ready access to legal information, they can participate fully in the affairs of their government. By collecting, organizing, preserving, and retrieving legal information, the members of the American Association of Law Libraries

---

[3] Robert M. Jarvis, "What Law Professors Will Want from Law Librarians in the Twenty-First Century," 96 *Law Library Journal* 503, 505 (Summer 2004).

[4] Susan Westerberg Prager, "Law Libraries and the Scholarly Mission," 96 *Law Library Journal* 513, 515 (Summer 2004).

enable people to make this ideal of democracy a reality."[5] Even fewer have first-hand experience to support such a sweeping claim. Indeed, most non-law librarians have not had occasion to ponder how "law firms, corporations, academic and governmental institutions, and the general public have legal information needs that are best addressed by professionals committed to the belief that serving these information needs is a noble calling."[6] Conveying such truths to "outsiders" and fostering a meaningful understanding of, and respect for, the work of law librarians remains one of the most pressing tasks for today's law school librarians.

How Are the Challenges Overcome?

The stakes are high in the battle for the future of academic law librarianship. The issue is not whether the profession will survive, but what it will look like. Accordingly, the profession must be proactive in combating perceptions with reality. One obvious strategy in this situation is to develop a unifying vision that better defines law librarianship within academia. For example, the natural sciences, the social sciences, and the humanities and fine arts can be viewed as groups of disciplines that study and build upon a body of substantive knowledge. Without digressing into a discussion of where law fits among these fields,[7] it is worth noting that much of law librarianship is dedicated to preserving, organizing, and disseminating the substantive works of the legal profession. In this context, librarians can be seen as possessing what could loosely be called "procedural," rather than substantive, knowledge. Instead of the abstract higher planes of intellectual exercise that characterize the substantive areas, librarians find themselves pigeonholed as the mere stewards of what the substantive areas produce. However, it is important to note that without the procedural there could be

---

[5] American Association of Law Libraries Ethical Principles, retrieved March 24, 2008, at www.aallnet.org/about/policy_ethics.asp.

[6] American Association of Law Libraries Ethical Principles, retrieved March 24, 2008, at www.aallnet.org/about/policy_ethics.asp.

[7] Interestingly, the forefather of modern legal education vehemently argued that the study of law was closely related to the natural sciences group. Christopher Columbus Langdell (b. 1826, d. 1906, dean of Harvard Law School, 1870–1895) believed the law existed to be discovered empirically through scientific inquiry, investigation, and experimentation. In his view, the law library was directly analogous to the chemist's laboratory. Today, in light of the increasingly interdisciplinary nature of law, some might argue that the social sciences offer a better "fit" for the legal profession.

no substantive. Substantive progress requires the ability to "stand on the shoulders of giants" and build upon the work of others. Without this, each generation would start anew—progressing no further than the last. Therefore, librarians and their procedural skill set are obviously integral to the success of the substantive enterprise. Without them, the substantive areas would flounder. They would be cut off from each other and unable to effectively communicate over time and geography.

The intertwined nature of procedural and substantive knowledge is well illustrated by the role law librarians play in legal education. Academic law librarians have traditionally provided crucial components of most law school educations. In academia, the practical skills law librarians cultivate in legal research classes (and that most employers crave) have always been subordinate to the abstract realm of substantive courses. While there are movements advocating less theoretical law school curricula, this reality is unlikely to change anytime soon. Rather than tilting at that windmill, academic law librarians should focus their efforts upon promoting the positive attributes they bring to the table. This strategy dictates that law librarianship should continue and expand its efforts to highlight its relationship to education in general. What does a degree in education mean? It means the holder knows how to teach others substantive knowledge. Furthermore, the best educators teach their students how to learn on their own—they show their students how to effectively continue to learn substantive knowledge throughout their lifetimes. In the same way, librarians exist to show their students, clients, and patrons the procedures necessary to learn and utilize substantive knowledge. If this analogy can be more successfully demonstrated and nurtured, the future of librarianship will be much brighter.

The crucial leadership role of scholarship cannot be ignored as a component of this mission. Future scholarship must continue to emphasize the connection of law librarianship to legal education. This connection is perhaps best illustrated by the dynamic state of modern legal research, largely driven by the electronic revolution. The entrenched print paradigm has been uprooted by electronic research resources, bringing new considerations and challenges to the forefront. Legal research guru Robert C. Berring has identified the "key questions for those concerned about legal information in the twenty-first century" as "What constitutes legal information, who controls it, and how is it changing?"[8] Academic law librarians must continue to cultivate scholarship that puts them at the forefront of these issues.

The subject of scholarship is an extremely important one because, perhaps more than anything else, the imperative to publish distinguishes academic law librarianship from law librarianship in general. The three components of a law school librarian's charge are the familiar teaching, scholarship, and service requirements that occupy traditional faculty members. While the proportions are necessarily shifted to emphasize professional performance for librarian faculty members, the necessity of scholarship to guide the profession cannot be overemphasized. It also offers the opportunity for law librarianship to develop its own body of substantive knowledge and overcome the limitations of a purely procedural orientation. There are many substantive issues that, thanks to their unique expertise, law librarians are uniquely suited to tackle. Some of the most obvious include matters of the First Amendment, copyright law, and media law. Ultimately, the benchmarks for success in law librarianship's quest for identity will include not only a thriving profession, but also many important contributions in these and other substantive areas of study.

Christopher L. Steadham is a 2004 graduate of the University of Kansas School of Law and a 2007 graduate of the master's of legal information management program offered through Emporia State University in conjunction with the University of Kansas School of Law. His primary responsibilities include conducting and coordinating legal and interdisciplinary research for the law school faculty and teaching legal research courses. He also writes a bimonthly literature review column for the Civic Research Institute and speaks at continuing legal education seminars on the subject of legal research.

Acknowledgment: *The author wishes to thank the many teachers, mentors, and colleagues who have guided the way on the path less traveled.*

---

[8] Richard A. Danner, "Contemporary and Future Directions in American Legal Research: Responding to the Threat of the Available," 31 *Int'l J. Legal Info.* 179, 188 (Summer 2003) citing Robert C. Berring, "Legal Information and the Search for Cognitive Authority," 88 *California Law Review* 1673, 1677–78 (2000).

The Impact of New Technology on Librarianship

Carol A. Parker

Law Library Director and Associate Professor of Law
University of New Mexico School of Law

ASPATORE
BOOKS

Technology and Teaching the Research Process

Before becoming a law library director for the University of New Mexico Law School in 2004, I was an assistant law library director at Wayne State University, and prior to that position I was the head of public services at Michigan State University College of Law. I was eager to accept the law library director position at my present school, because it also offered me the opportunity to teach extensively. I now teach advanced legal research, international legal research, and wills and trusts.

Teaching is one of the three key areas of this profession that have been most greatly impacted by the advent of new technologies and other research tools. In some ways, the introduction of online legal resources into the legal research process makes learning that process more challenging. I believe that despite the existence of online legal resources, legal researchers should still understand how to conduct research using print materials, because mastering that format contributes to an understanding of the basic structure of legal information, where it comes from, and how law-making entities organize that information. For example, all three branches of government at both the federal and state levels make law. In print, that law is always published in two formats: (1) a chronological record of the laws produced, and (2) a compilation of the current law arranged hierarchically by subject. It doesn't matter what law-making entity is involved. The primary law of that entity will always be accessible in print in those two formats, rather like the two sides of a coin. It makes sense at a fundamental level that lawmakers would want to maintain a historical chronological record of their work. That record is static and is never altered (e.g., the Federal Register). On the other hand, a researcher interested in accessing the current law must be able to access the law via a subject arrangement law (e.g., the Code of Federal Regulations), because otherwise you could never locate anything.

Today, virtually all primary law has migrated online. Primary law published in online databases and removed from the context of its print analog does not easily convey to the student researcher the more subtle differences between chronological and hierarchical subject arrangements. In the online environment, these two types of resources look very much the same. You can explain that the chronological and hierarchical subject arrangements have different purposes, but the differences between the two and how you use them to your advantage are much less obvious in the online environment. There is no substitute for showing a student a long expanse of print case law reporters in the library to emphasize the point about chronological arrangement, and then comparing that format to the hierarchical subject arrangement of case law available in print digests. For the fullest understanding of the legal research process, one will master both print and electronic resources, and one will know how to use both formats for maximum cost-effectiveness. I think the current situation of needing to master both formats makes it that much harder to learn how to do legal research. Consequently, law librarians have become much more involved in the teaching of the research process, and I think this trend will continue, because it is unlikely that research materials will become any less complicated in the near future.

In addition, there is now a national movement for legal education curricular reform that has the potential to significantly increase the need for law librarian teaching of legal research within law schools. Law schools across the country are taking a new look at how law students learn in light of recent work by the Carnegie Foundation for the Advancement of Teaching and the Clinical Legal Education Association. I envision that law librarians will be playing an important role in the curricular reform movement, because the best way to enable students to master the research technologies of today's law practice is by incorporating law librarians into the teaching process.

Digitization and Preservation of Library Materials

The other key way technology has affected what law librarians do is in the area of preservation and digitization of legal materials. Governments are not providing print publications of primary legal material as frequently as they used to. In fact, many government documents are now "born digital." There are many challenges to preserving official records of primary legal material that exist only online. Several organizations of law librarians are working to meet those challenges. For example, the American Association of Law Libraries recently conducted a survey of authenticated state material on the Web, which I believe represents a very significant contribution in this area. The survey seeks to answer the question of which states, if any, have adopted Web sites of primary legal material as official and authentic, thus effectively making those Web sites as authoritative as official print publications would have been in the past. As fewer states invest in producing official print publications, states must be encouraged to designate their Web site as official instead.

Aside from the authenticity of electronic resources, there are other challenges for libraries that might want to "go electronic." Ideally, we could maintain our print collections as well as acquire electronic resources, but in many cases, we simply cannot afford to have both print and electronic versions of library materials. Law school library budgets are increasingly limited, which means librarians often have to make some hard choices between formats—and in the rush to move online, that often comes at the expense of print and primary legal materials. Unfortunately, that also means we are at increased risk of no longer having a reliable print record of primary legal materials.

Several groups are now working on the challenge of preserving print primary materials, lest they be discarded in haste to move online, including initiatives being undertaken by the Legal Information Preservation Alliance, the Law Library Microfilm Consortium, and the Desert States Law Library Consortium. I am personally involved in a regional preservation initiative undertaken by the Desert States Law Library Consortium, a group of ten law schools in the Southwest that is working to designate print copies of last resort for our states' pre-statehood and primary legal materials (e.g., constitutions, session laws, cases, and administrative regulations). For example, our school's law library will be the repository of New Mexico primary materials. We would preserve that material and designate it as part of this repository, and pledge to make it available to our other member libraries, which could then safely discard their own copies of New Mexico primary materials, knowing our copies have been set aside to preserve that record. The process of inventorying this material will also lead to a database of information that can be drawn upon to make decisions about historical material that should be digitized to increase assess for researchers. Establishing similar repositories in other libraries also ameliorates the risk of loss of access to primary materials that is associated with relying solely on commercial database vendors as greater numbers of law libraries move toward electronic access at the expense of print.

Looking to the future, I believe law school libraries will need to continue to expand their efforts to preserve and digitize historical legal materials. I personally like to apply the slogan of the green movement to the decision of what to preserve or digitize—"think globally, act locally." I certainly have no reason to digitize something that is widely available nationally. But there is a lot of material unique to New Mexico (e.g., material related to Spanish and Mexican land grants that were awarded by those governments to residents of what eventually became the state of New Mexico), and I believe libraries can make a big contribution by digitizing those types of materials in order to make them accessible twenty-four hours a day, seven days a week, worldwide. Previously, no one would have had access to unique New Mexico materials unless they physically traveled to our state. In addition, the process of digitization helps preserve such material, because we can keep the print original in our rare book room, and researchers do not have to handle it to have access to the material.

Librarians as Publishers

A third trend in law libraries made possible by new technology is that of the librarian as publisher via the use of online institutional repositories. Institutional repositories are essentially servers that store and make freely available on the Web, digital collections that capture and preserve a law school's intellectual output. It is usually the law librarians who develop and maintain such repositories within law schools. Institutional repositories can be used to disseminate and promote legal scholarship. In addition, they provide an important means to access material not traditionally published elsewhere, such as student scholarship, teaching material, and original documents uncovered during the course of scholarly research.

Law faculties come into possession of important original documents in the course of their work, gather large amounts of background material, and conduct empirical research. The potential for institutional repositories to disseminate important material that would otherwise languish in a file cabinet is one of the most exciting applications emerging from the development of institutional repositories. Faculty with access to an institutional repository can essentially become publishers without having to go through an information technology department. We should not overlook the contribution that could be made if law faculties digitized and shared original research materials in addition to the articles they ultimately create from them, and law librarians are facilitating these advances.

For example, the law faculty at the University of New Mexico School of Law uses its institutional repository to disseminate material that would otherwise not be published. One member of the law faculty published the 1974 transcript of a federal district court trial that led to a U.S. Supreme Court opinion affirming tribal sovereignty. Another is publishing not only reports, but also previously unpublished meeting transcripts from the 1998 Western Water Policy Review Advisory Commission she chaired. A third has published a clinic civil practice manual, thus sharing it with the public as well as making it permanently available for clinic students. A fourth published updating material for a bankruptcy treatise. These materials are now all discoverable via Internet search engines, and the faculty members can share these documents with colleagues simply by sharing the Web addresses.

Law schools can use institutional repositories to publish student papers, legal theses, and dissertations in institutional repositories. Access to this material has previously been scanty, because it was rarely published and even more rarely indexed. Print collections, where they existed, were created by binding and cataloging the material for local collections. Law schools that create digital collections of these works can make them available to the world at large. Making student scholarship available in digital collections provides students with a continuing connection to their school after graduation. Knowing their work will also be subject to scrutiny beyond the four walls of their professors' offices would also give law students added incentive to produce better scholarship.

Key Traits of Today's Successful Law School Librarian

I believe today's law school librarian must be capable of continually reinventing himself or herself. If you do not keep your skills up to date, you will fall behind in this field, and that includes technological skills. There is much change occurring in today's law school library, largely because there is much change occurring within the overall legal education environment. Therefore, participation in continuing education programs such as those provided by library consortia and national organizations (like the American

Association of Law Libraries and its many regional chapters and sections) is critical. Library consortia in particular have become adept at using technology for continuing education, and we are seeing many more webinars and other online or distance education technologies being available to help law librarians keep current. For example, the Online Computer Library Center now offers a wide array of webinars on topics like podcasting, Web 2.0 tools, virtual reference, cataloging, and collection analysis tools.

Challenges for Today's Law School Librarians

A law school librarian has to anticipate that what they are doing at the beginning of their career is likely going to be far different than what they will be doing near the end of their career. Therefore, I think it helps if you also have a flexible personality—if you are a person who does not like change, this may not be the right field for you at this particular time. Being flexible goes beyond keeping up with new technology, because it is not just the technology in this field that is going to change, but also the work a librarian will end up doing. Law school librarians will always be challenged to spend their budget wisely in terms of putting information resources in place, but the challenge going forward is likely to include providing the proper gateway to the user to help them make use of the library's resources—and the process of providing that gateway is likely to change quite a bit in the years to come.

Indeed, along with all of the recent advances in technology, there is still a basic need for the user to be able to access that information—and librarians remain involved in the access process despite widespread availability of online databases. For example, consider the seemingly simple decision to cancel a print loose-leaf title (a title that is manually updated by regularly replacing outdated pages to keep the content current), and instead subscribe to the continually current online version of that title because it will eliminate the labor involved in manual updating. While that may seem like a very logical business decision, every person who was accustomed to using the print loose-leaf will now have to learn how to navigate the online interface instead. The labor involved with the title is shifted from updating the print copy to training patrons how to use the online version. As a result of decisions like this, today's law librarians often end up providing a lot of teaching and legal research instruction on a one-to-one basis from the reference desk—and that process can be incredibly challenging, because library users have all different levels of skill with respect to navigating a computer online interface.

Therefore, one of the greatest challenges of the last few years has been the need for librarians to help patrons figure out how to access research material online, and that is related to the expanded role for librarians in the overall teaching process. Research is more complicated these days, and there is a much greater role for librarians in terms of teaching not just law students, but all of the attorneys and other patrons who come to the library.

Primary Goals of a Law School Librarian

The primary objectives and goals of a law school librarian will be determined by the primary goals of the law school library they work in— and the law school itself. Therefore, law school librarians will have diverse goals, simply because law school libraries are so diverse. Every library has some basic commonalities, but their missions can vary greatly. For example, at the University of New Mexico Law Library, we are the only large academic law library in the state. Therefore, our library has to serve the needs of our faculty and students, as well as the bar and the bench, and the public. In fact, about 45 percent of the questions we take at the reference desk are from the public (not counting what we do for faculty, which is tabulated separately). Law libraries with other missions may have very different goals for their institution.

In terms of commonalities among law school libraries of primary goals, there is always an obligation to be wise money managers. As previously noted, law library budgets are in many cases shrinking—they are rarely growing—and legal resources are getting very expensive. Therefore, as a law school librarian, you have to be a careful manager of the money that is entrusted to you, because law schools can invest a significant percentage of their budgets in their libraries, depending on the overall size.

Law school librarians must also be prepared, first and foremost, to serve the needs of their faculty and students. An area of service that has really expanded recently in law libraries is the extent to which law librarians are providing faculty research support. This used to be a service that only large, well-funded libraries provided, but I think there is now an expectation among most law faculties that librarians will be available to help them with their research. Here at the University of New Mexico, we have worked very hard over the last five years to promote the message that our librarians are happy to help the faculty with their research. We have substantially increased what we are doing for the faculty, and I have pledged several librarians to that effort. The services we offer are typical of the trend in this area. We currently provide faculty research assistance, book and article delivery, individualized database assistance and training, e-mail alerting and routed material, guest lectures on research for law school classes, research assistant training, and an institutional repository for online publishing of faculty scholarship and teaching materials.

Although our school has a small faculty of only thirty-five, in a typical year the law library will complete about 350 research requests and more than 1,000 deliveries of requested items. To manage this high volume of work, we use a custom-designed, password-protected database for initiating and managing faculty requests. The database automatically routes the request to the appropriate individual for action. Faculty members may also use the Web site to monitor the progress of requests. The Web-based service request form associated with the database may be used to initiate all of the services offered. Typically, the librarians gather and review (but not synthesize or analyze) materials to complete research requests. They also provide a memorandum summarizing the research process (e.g., where looked, what found, online queries used, etc.) so a project can be updated easily or continued in the future by others. The librarians are also available for personal consultation with faculty members regarding new resources that might be available for various projects. The library hires law students to assist them with faculty research support, especially for projects that do not require a quick turnaround. Working in the law library offers students another opportunity to acquire the research skills to prepare them for legal practice. Librarians are also available to train a faculty member's personal research assistants and serve as consultants for them.

In addition, more faculty research is becoming interdisciplinary, which can be challenging, because that often means you will be called upon to provide resources from subjects a law library would not normally collect, or to support empirical research, which is a growing trend among law faculties. Therefore, it is very important for law school librarians to collaborate with other specialized libraries, as well as large university libraries if possible. Indeed, I think it is a great advantage if a law school library is associated with a university library, because it can then draw on the substantial resources of such a library. Simply stated, if you are able to cultivate partnerships or collaborations with other libraries, you can call on your colleagues at those other institutions to provide material you do not have or cannot afford. I believe it is vitally important for law school libraries to reach out and build bridges to other libraries—and a law library that acts monolithically does so at its own peril.

Benchmarks for Success

I personally love collecting statistics, and I am constantly trying to quantify our gains in resources and services. Whenever I undertake a new initiative, I will take a bench line measurement and I will then re-quantify the project at least annually. For example, before undertaking a vigorous campaign to increase faculty research support, I would recommend that you quantify the level of support you currently offer. That way, you can measure later on and will hopefully be able to show a quantifiable increase in service provided. Because of my preference for collecting data, I now have years' worth of rich and informative data to draw upon as needed. For example, when I am meeting with the law school deans or faculty, or when I am at alumni or community events, it is incredibly useful to be able to pull out statistics that show the impact of our library. I will also frequently work those statistics into marketing materials and brochures. I may point to an increased use of our Web site by a certain percentage over the course of the year that might be attributable to an outreach initiative, or if I write a thank-you letter to a donor who has contributed money to the law library, I will say, "It is because of donations such as yours that we are able to answer X number of questions at the reference desk or circulate X number of books over the course of a year." I measure everything I can think of, and it has really made a difference in terms of my ability to get the message out about the importance of our library.

Indeed, I believe that if you do not have some way to quantify what you do, your achievements will be largely unknown to both the general public and the law school faculty and administration. For example, if I can say to the faculty, "We doubled the amount of our faculty research support in the past two years," I will get a much more positive reaction than if I merely say, "We are doing a lot more to support faculty research." Simply stated, you must be able to craft a consistent and appropriate message about what the library is doing and how it can help others, and then deliver it at the appropriate time. In other words, you have to prepare sound bites for those "elevator" moments.

I used sound bites effectively several years ago at another school when I was trying to get the school to commit to allowing its faculty research assistant budget to be used to pay for a pool of librarian-supervised research assistants. One day I had an unexpected opportunity to plead my case when I ran into the law school dean in the elevator. Fortunately, I had my sound bite at the ready. I said to the dean, "Please let the faculty spend their research budget on research assistants that work for the librarians rather than directly for the faculty," and I explained why that would make sense. You must have your message prepared, because you never know when you are going to get an opportunity to promote a project.

Helpful Resources

I am always ready to look outside to supplement the talent I have in-house, because at any given moment I might need expertise to help me with a new project. For example, I might need to hire an archivist because the current trend toward preservation often leads to the need to create archival collections. I may also need to hire a disaster planning expert to update my emergency response manual, or I may need to hire a marketing specialist if I want to undertake a new outreach program. If I want to create a positive opportunity for all of the staff to come together outside of work and get to know each other better, I may decide to call on communications experts or consultants in the human resources field to come in and facilitate that process. If we need to move some portions of the collection to other locations, I will hire movers rather than expect the staff to do it. Indeed, the list of outside resources a law librarian may need to call on never ends. And in terms of a cost/benefit analysis, you are often better off even canceling some titles, if necessary, to get the funds to hire any experts you need. I believe it is always better to hire experts to do what they do best, rather than trying to get your library staff to do the job, because they will never do it as well.

My willingness to make use of outside resources may stem from the fact that I was fortunate to work at Wayne State University for several years early in my career. That law library is unlike most other academic law libraries—it is part of the university library system, and it is not under the administration of the law school. That job provided my first real exposure to working closely with the professional librarians at a main library, a health sciences library, and a science library, which helped me realize the wisdom of reaching out to other library communities when possible. I found that experts in other libraries can offer tremendous knowledge and resources, and they are generally happy to share them and/or partner with you for collaborative purchases and other projects. Larger libraries have resources I will never have in our small library, consisting of only six librarians and me. We simply cannot build the expertise in various areas we are bound to need. Unfortunately, I sometimes see a tendency for law librarians to first look inward and think, "If we need to do something with this archive, one of us should become an archivist," rather than hiring a consultant or reaching out to an archivist at another library or school.

Difficulties of the Changing Role

Perhaps the most difficult aspect of this job in recent times pertains to print collection management, because this area is in great flux at present. Librarians are increasingly cutting their print resources—sometimes by choice, because they feel it is beneficial to convert their services to an electronic format, and sometimes out of necessity, because the budget has been cut and something has to go. Some libraries may choose to do rolling updates of key treatises on a quarterly or annual basis, rather than investing in continuous updates, or they may even choose to update some treatises only once every two to three years, because it may be cheaper in some instances to discard an outdated treatise and buy a replacement copy every two or three years, rather than continuously updating a title over the same period of time (the researcher experiences some inconvenience as a result, but he or she would have had to check their research for currency in any case). However, such a strategy can be very challenging to implement, because libraries' procedures are typically structured around continuous, not periodical updating. That is just one example of the challenges involved in trying to maintain print collections in an era where such collections are contracting, and all of our policies and procedures have been built around maintenance, if not growth.

Another challenge comes from turnover in librarians on staff. Librarians will frequently leave to go on to new opportunities and promotions, or to retire from the profession. We recently experienced several retirements. Therefore, it is getting more common to see many years' worth of knowledge of a collection walk out the door when someone leaves. Unfortunately, this trend is unlikely to change. However, these challenges are not unique to law libraries. The same challenges can be found across all departments of academia, and in the business arena as well.

Final Thoughts

I believe this profession has been and will continue to be one of the best jobs in the world. While we face many challenges, the abilities of professional librarians are so strong that I believe we are going to meet all of those challenges. It is going to be exciting to see the outcome of the trends that are now facing this profession, because challenges create opportunities—and librarians have the opportunity to mold and shape the outcome of the challenges they are facing.

Professor Carol A. Parker became the director of the University of New Mexico School of Law Library in 2004, leaving behind a position as assistant director at the Wayne State University Law Library. Before that, she served as the head of faculty and public services in the Law Library at the Michigan State University College of Law. She teaches wills and trusts, advanced legal research, and international legal research at the University of New Mexico School of Law. She previously taught advanced legal research and legal research, writing, and advocacy at Michigan State University.

We Are in the
Business of Service:
Serving Students and Faculty
in an Academic Law Library

Olivia Leigh Weeks

Director of the Law Library and Assistant Professor of Law
Campbell University,
Norman Adrian Wiggins School of Law

Oddly enough, the first law library collections were entrusted to students, janitors, and old men. The only qualification for serving as a law librarian was that one did not require a large salary. Christine A. Brock, "Law Libraries and Librarians: A Revisionist History; or More Than You Ever Wanted to Know," 67 *Law Libr. J.* 325 (1974). This was indicative of the fact that "the position of a law librarian was regarded as requiring no particular talent." Massey, "Law School Administration and the Law Librarian," 10 *J. Legal Ed.* 215, 221 (1957). Over time, this has changed. Now most professional law librarians hold not only a degree in library science, but a law degree as well. The dual degrees give law librarians the educational background they need to serve their patrons with knowledge and skill.

Law librarians fulfill an important role, because the academic law library is the intellectual heart of the law school. It is where research and learning take place for faculty, students, staff, and members of the bench and bar. Over the years, the role of librarianship has evolved in many ways. Librarians are now administrators, teachers, and managers. In addition, librarians have become very specialized in the services they provide. No longer does one librarian tend to circulation duties, assist students with research, and perform reference services for faculty. Most law libraries now have circulation, reference, and faculty services librarians in addition to librarians who handle acquisitions, collection development, and cataloging. All of these librarians support the law school by providing services that have a direct impact on the faculty and students.

Over the past few years, librarians have also had to become computer-literate and technologically savvy. They have had to learn many different types of technologies to stay abreast of what is going on not only in the publishing world, but also in the world of electronic legal resources. In addition, the arrival of technology has changed the way librarians teach legal research and assist faculty and students in their research efforts.

One of our responsibilities as librarians is to prepare our students for the day they will practice law. Therefore, the influx of technology has had a major impact on the way we teach students. Primarily, we have to make sure that when we work with students, we give them a proper background not only in the printed format, but also in understanding how to use the electronic resources that are now available, so when they go out to practice—regardless of whether they work in a one-person law firm that relies predominantly on printed materials, or whether they go into a multi-lawyer firm that relies mostly on electronic resources—they can work in either type of work environment and do so competently. It is the goal of every librarian to teach students how to do efficient, cost-effective research in whatever format the student chooses to use.

Using Print Materials versus Electronic Resources

Surprisingly, there are some types of research that are actually much easier, faster, and more cost-effective to perform using printed materials rather than electronic resources. It is the responsibility of librarians to teach students the most efficient, cost- effective way of conducting their research. For example, it is much easier to go to the shelf and pull the index to a state code, look in the index, and then go to the provision than it is to go online and find the same information. Indeed, many of the students I teach will come to me and say, "You were right about using the statutes in printed format. It is so much easier, because you have all the provisions laid out for you in such a way that you can easily go from one provision to the other." When the same statutes are presented online, each provision may be presented on a single screen page, and a user will have to flip from screen to screen to read the entire relevant section or chapter.

Printed resources are also valuable for doing background research. Many times students have difficulty doing research because they are not familiar with the area of law or simply need a review of a specific area. What they need is an overview of the law and references to cases, law reviews, or other materials that address the issues they are researching. In this situation, a hornbook or treatise is typically the place to go—and it is much easier and more cost-effective to read the information in printed format than online.

At the same time, there are other situations where the use of online resources is much easier, faster, and more cost-effective. For example, if a student is looking for a U.S. Supreme Court opinion that was handed down within the past twenty-four hours, the only place the full opinion can be found is through an online service. If the researcher knows the name of the case, the subject matter, or the parties involved, he or she can quickly locate the case online. This is a very efficient and cost-effective use of online resources.

Online resources are also a cost-effective way to update information. For example, when you are doing research, one of the steps you take is to update any cases or statutes you are using. If you are relying on a particular case in your work, you want to know if that case is still good law or if it has been cited positively by other courts. If you are relying on a particular statute, you want to know if the statute has been repealed or amended. The best resource for updating either of these sources is an online citatory, because an online citator updates this type of information on a daily basis, and these frequent updates enable students and faculty to always stay on top of what is happening with a particular case or statute.

As librarians, we want our students and faculty to be aware of the many resources available to them, and to know how to use them. We would be remiss if we focused on teaching our students and faculty the value of resources in one format while completely ignoring resources in the many other formats available. Therefore, it is our responsibility to expose our patrons to all of the resources at their fingertips, educate them as to the strengths and weaknesses of each, and show how the many types of resources complement each other. Some resources are not available in print format. By the same token, resources may be available in print format and not readily available electronically. Therefore, one type of research resource often complements the other, and every student and faculty member should know what resource to use for the best results.

Meeting Patron Needs

Our law library's mission is "to play the leading role in meeting the information needs of the law school community, to provide comprehensive information resources and services to advance legal scholarship, and to support the curriculum and programs of the law school, the university, and the bench and bar." Guided by its mission, the law library is committed to the goal of providing for its users a library that is active in the educational life of the law school and responsive to the educational and research needs of the faculty, staff, and students. Our main concern in fulfilling this goal is to provide support for both the mission and the directives of the law school.

One of the goals of the law library is to provide services to advance legal scholarship, and to support the curriculum and programs of the law school. To encourage people to use the library and avail themselves of its services, the library should be a place where patrons want to frequent. It should be a warm, welcoming, and inviting place for students and faculty to do research, study, and learn. In addition, the library staff should always be available to assist patrons with their research and reference needs.

An academic law library provides services that support both faculty and student needs, whether that entails helping them obtain inter-library loans or showing them how to use a new database that has been recently acquired. Simply put, our focus is to support the faculty, students, and, to a lesser degree, members of the bench and bar. Our goal is to provide the finest legal resources and services possible.

To provide these services, today's law school librarian has to have an intimate working knowledge of the library's collections and be skilled at using the electronic resources owned or subscribed to by the library. This is not always easy, since some electronic resources are easier to use than others are. Most libraries subscribe to multiple electronic services, and the search methods for using each varies in differing degrees. The more sophisticated and specialized the service, the more complicated are the research strategies. For example, key word searches may be effectively used in some databases, while Boolean searches are more effective in others, and it is much easier to teach students how to do a key word search than it is to teach them to use Boolean logic to structure a search.

In addition, librarians must have a strong working knowledge of the electronic resources so they will be skilled enough to communicate this information not only to the students, but to the faculty as well. The research needs of the faculty are different from those of law students, and the levels of computer competency vary among members of the faculty. As a result, an important service of the library is to inform faculty members of the multiple electronic sources that are available to them and how various sources can support their research efforts. Even when the faculty becomes aware of these resources, some will be hesitant to use the resources, or they will not feel comfortable using any type of online service. Some faculty members prefer to use printed resources, and their experience with online services is limited. Therefore, it is our responsibility as librarians to inform the faculty about all the resources the library offers, be available to answer questions about specific sources, and be prepared to teach them how to use the resources that will benefit their research agendas. Sometimes a librarian must have patience as well as the skill to be effective.

Another important service a library provides to its patrons is teaching them how to use various resources in informal workshops. Workshops can focus on a multitude of subjects—everything from advanced online research to how to use loose-leaf services. These informal workshops can be a very effective way of introducing faculty and students to new online services. They can also be an effective way to offer review sessions to students on specific types of legal research, or to prepare students for their first summer clerkship.

Although informal workshops can be very effective, we must also be willing to work individually with any library patrons who are hesitant to participate on that level. It is extremely important in this changing environment to focus on the patrons and their needs, and to find the most effective way of meeting those needs, whether in an informal classroom setting, a computer lab, or an office.

In addition, most professional library staffs are involved and will continue to be involved in making classroom presentations at the request of faculty members. Many of the classroom presentations are focused on teaching students about resources available in a specialized area of law, and then helping students formulate effective research strategies for finding the information they need for papers or projects. The staff's direct involvement with students in the classroom helps establish a rapport with the students that results in students seeking out librarians for assistance in research and writing projects.

Law librarians are in the business of providing services and resources to their patrons that enhance research efforts, support the curriculum, and support the missions of both the library and the law school. We are committed to serving the legal information needs of the law school, the university, and the bench and bar.

Challenges for Today's Law School Librarians

One of the biggest challenges law school librarians are currently facing is the rising cost of legal materials. The cost of materials in printed format is increasing every year, and so are the costs of electronic resources—and of course, we have limited budgets. Therefore, there often comes a point where libraries have to decide whether to cancel some of their print subscriptions in order to add additional electronic resources, or continue to select the print resources and forego the electronic. You walk a fine line in making these decisions. The library wants to provide its faculty and students with the finest legal resources available in the format they will use, but at the same time, it needs to have a balanced mixture of formats for students and faculty.

Indeed, one of the most difficult decisions for a law school librarian is deciding where that line is—how many print resources do you keep, or how many do you cancel in order to provide more access to electronic resources? Many law library materials are now available in electronic format as well as printed format, which means we often wind up duplicating certain sources, which in most cases is not cost-effective. For example, we are a North Carolina law school. Therefore, it is important that we have an extensive collection of North Carolina materials, both primary and secondary. Some of these materials are only available in print, and this makes a purchasing decision easy. Other North Carolina sources are available in both print and electronic resources. Do we purchase both or subscribe to only one? Again, the answer is easy: we purchase both because we want to offer our patrons an in-depth collection of North Carolina materials. Of course, an extensive North Carolina collection would not hold the same importance for out-of-state law libraries, and the North Carolina materials available on Westlaw and Lexis would fulfill their research needs. Westlaw and Lexis provide access to both primary and secondary materials from every jurisdiction, and they are relied on to provide access to primary legal materials not owned by a library. In fact, every law student is trained to use each system, because one or the other (sometimes both) are subscribed to by law firms.

An academic law library is constantly trying to support the mission of the law school, which entails providing the materials that will support the curriculum and research agendas of the faculty and students. Therefore, purchasing decisions are evaluated from a number of different angles, and several different factors are incorporated into the evaluation to determine which format will best serve the law school, the faculty, and the students. All academic law libraries have a collection development policy for selection according to format. For example, the following policy outlines the criteria that may be used for format selection:

> As the result of changing technology, legal information is now available in a wide variety of formats (microforms, books, online databases, CD-ROMs, the Internet, CDs, video cassettes, and DVDs). Each of these formats present advantages and disadvantages for patron service and collection building. In determining the appropriate format for selection, the following are guidelines to be used:
>
> - Authoritativeness of content
> - Ease of access
> - Readability
> - Storage considerations
> - Longevity of format
> - Currency of information
> - Potential historical significance
>
> The large-scale computerization of legal information sources has led to the increased use and reliance on electronic databases as primary sources of information. Many primary and secondary sources are now available in electronic format, as well as in print. The criteria used to determine the appropriate mix of traditional and electronic resources include:
>
> - When the price of publication versus use is too high
> - Multiple copies/duplicate subscriptions
> - Lesser-used sets

- Titles that can be reinstated if there is a need
- "User-friendly" product

"Collection Development Policy," Norman Adrian Wiggins School of Law Library (2008)

The collection development policy guidelines give the library's collection development committee standards by which to evaluate materials being considered for purchase. The policy also provides guidelines for determining titles that can be canceled.

Key Skills and Training for Today's Law School Librarians

Today's law school librarians must be service-oriented. They must always be aware of the needs of their patrons—and in the case of a law school, our master patron group consists of our faculty and students. Librarians also need to be able to use their time effectively and efficiently, because we are called upon to do so many duties. Indeed, in most law schools, you typically have one librarian responsible for many different duties. For example, the director of the library is responsible for overseeing the library budget, managing staff, collection development, and overseeing the provision of services to faculty and staff. In addition, he or she may teach legal research and writing, a substantive course. Therefore, time management is a key skill that librarians as well as other professionals have to learn.

As a law school librarian, you also have to learn how to prioritize your goals and objectives. Sometimes we get caught up in trivial matters and forget our primary goals and objectives. Therefore, we must evaluate the importance of each task, the deadline for completing each task, and arrange them according to the ultimate goal we are trying to achieve.

A law school librarian must also be able to do strategic planning in terms of setting both long-term and short-term goals, and he or she must be able to set timelines by which the short-term goals will be completed. For example, our library has to put a security system in place within the next eighteen months. Therefore, the long-term goal is to have a functioning security system in place by that date. The short-term goals are:

- Meet with vendors whose security systems are compatible with the library's integrated library system.
- Evaluate the pros and cons of each system and make a decision within the month.
- Divide the collection into sections, and prioritize the order in which the books in that section are to be tagged.
- Train members of the library staff.
- Hire and train student workers.
- Assign teams to tag specific areas of the collection.
- Set up a schedule for the tagging process.

It is helpful if timelines can be set for the completion of each short-term goal. However, flexibility is the key. Rarely are goals completed within the set time, especially when working on a project of this magnitude.

If you do not have the training or the skills to set long-term and short-term goals, you can become overwhelmed by a project, or certain things may get left by the wayside. Therefore, it is a good idea to take the time on the front end of a project to do the planning that is necessary to carry out the project efficiently. You need to work with your staff so each staff member knows exactly what the project entails, what is going on, what they are responsible for each step of the way, and the timeline within which each of their responsibilities must be met. This type of planning helps ensure that you will have both a happier staff and a more successful project. I have always found that a library staff is much more willing to work on a project if you meet with them at the outset and make them an integral part of the decision-making and planning. Indeed, it is important for librarians to learn to work with their staff and make them part of whatever goes on within the library. If the staff feels as if they have ownership in what is going on, they will take pride in what they do.

Of course, it is also necessary for a law librarian to have the proper credentials and training for his or her position. A master's degree in library science is essential for the professional law school librarian. Reference librarians also need a law degree. Their duties require knowledge of the law as well as the skills of librarianship. Of course, reference librarians must also have strong research skills. On the other hand, a law library director must have strong management skills, because that individual is managing not only a staff, but also a budget and all of the components that make up a law school library. Most importantly, all librarians should enjoy working with people, because people are our business—ultimately our first priority is to serve our patrons.

In addition, teaching skills are a bonus for a law librarian. Most law schools typically have a first-year research and writing course, and in many schools, the law librarians participate in the teaching of this course. Teaching in a first-year course helps establish a good working rapport between the students and the library staff. However, teaching is not restricted to the classroom. Teaching is done informally every day of the week. As a librarian, you must teach library users about the materials you have in your library, how to use them, and where to find them. And in that process, all of a librarian's skills come into play. Some of these skills come from formal education, and some from experience. The better a librarian knows the collection, the more a librarian teaches, and the more interaction a librarian has with the patrons, the better he or she will become at doing this job and doing it well.

Communicating the Library's Resources

One of the most important tasks of a law school librarian is to inform faculty and students about the resources their library currently offers or may be offering in the future. For example, if we are considering the purchase of an electronic resource, the company or vendor representative will generally give us a free trial. We will then e-mail our faculty to let them know we are considering this resource, and we would like them to use it and give us their feedback. Once we purchase a particular electronic resource, we will again send e-mails to our faculty letting them know we have purchased the resource. We will explain what materials are available on the database or service, and remind them that the library staff members are available to train them to use the service.

We also send e-mails to our students on a regular basis to let them know about the services we offer. We conduct workshops where we invite students and/or faculty to train on particular electronic resources. We also let our faculty and students know what new printed materials we have added to the library each month. We send out an acquisition list as an e-mail attachment, and we put that information on our library's Web page.

If we add a new database to our collection, our library's home page will have a blurb featuring information about the service's content, instruction for accessing the material, and information regarding passwords and user names. In addition, we will include a direct link to that resource. Indeed, both faculty and students can go to our Web page and get instant updates about any new resources we have added to the library's collection.

We also put our old exams online to assist our students in their studies, and several weeks before exams, we send all of the students an e-mail reminding them that the old exams are online, how they can access them, and the password they will need to retrieve them. In addition, we subscribe to databases that are particularly helpful to students, and several times during the semester we will e-mail the student body to remind them this service is available and how to access it, and we let them know that if they are getting ready to study for exams, they will find these materials most helpful.

We also provide brochures for attorneys, students, and other library users to inform them of the library services and resources that are available to them. For example, we provide a document delivery service for attorneys. Through this service, we provide the attorneys with copies of cases or law review articles as long as their requests comply with copyright law. Members of the bar are invited to use our library, and we will provide reference assistance to any attorneys or members of their staff when they use our facilities. In addition, we provide many types of helpful research guides for our students and other patrons. (See Appendices D, E, and F.) We provide a location guide to the most used materials. All guides and brochures are kept at the circulation desk where they are easily accessible. It is amazing how many of these brochures and guides we distribute each year.

In a nutshell, we try to constantly update information about the library and the services it provides. We frequently remind our faculty and students with respect to what library resources are available, how those resources can be used, and how the resources can support their research, and we try to do so in a timely manner.

The Changing Library Budget

In the last four years, our electronic resources budget has increased dramatically to allow us to purchase materials that will enable our students to have access to the same electronic resources other law schools give their students. Consequently, our graduating students are just as competitive in the marketplace as students from larger schools. By subscribing to electronic resources and purchasing digital collections, we can give our faculty and students access to materials we could not purchase in printed format, either because we could not afford them or, if they are older scholarly treatises, because we may not be able to find them.

We are a relatively young law school in that we were founded in 1976. Therefore, we do not have the collection a much older law school would have. Investing in electronic resources has been a great way for us to be able to give our patrons access to a great field of knowledge.

Just as our budget has increased dramatically in the area of electronic resources, book budgets have also gone up, simply because the costs of legal materials have gone up dramatically. The increase in the book budget barely covers the cost of the continuations we receive each year, and very little is left for the purchase of new titles. Therefore, we rely on the library's collection development policy to guide us in the selection of materials to be added to the collection. Collection development is a collaborative effort involving members of the library staff (the collection development committee) as well as faculty and students. The collection development committee focuses on selecting materials that will support the curriculum as well as the scholarly research of the faculty. When selecting titles, the committee looks at the format—is it a loose-leaf service requiring frequent updates, a treatise that is updated annually, or monograph that requires no updating—the initial cost, as well as the annual cost of updating. Currently we are concentrating on collecting scholarly monographs that will give depth to our existing collection. In addition, the library tries to fulfill any requests submitted by the faculty.

Five Basic Steps to Navigating Our Changing Role

The first step is to identify and capitalize on your unique strengths and use those strengths to an advantage. At the same time, it is important to recognize the strengths of others and understand that those strengths may differ from yours. Then use your strengths and the strengths of others to work together as a team.

The second step is to expand your ability to do strategic planning. What are your goals for the future? How do you want to accomplish those goals? Formulate a strategic plan to accomplish these goals, in both the long and short term, including specific steps and timelines for accomplishing each goal.

The third step is to increase your capacity for creativity, innovation, and fresh ideas, and to be open to new ideas and concepts from other members of the profession. Continue to develop professionally and stay on top of new developments in the profession by attending conferences and workshops, and participating in online webinars.

The fourth step is to work effectively with the younger student generation as well as the varied personalities represented by the faculty. To be effective as a librarian, you must be able to communicate and work with the patrons you serve.

The fifth and final step is to embrace change rather than fight it. The role of the law librarian is constantly evolving, as is the world of information in which we work.

Changing Library Technologies

In recent years, we have certainly seen an increasing number of materials being made available in electronic format, and we are seeing more libraries digitizing special collections and making them more easily and readily assessable to patrons. Within the last three years, our library has been wired for wireless networking. All of the tables in the library now have electric outlets so students can use their laptops in the library. As a result, we no longer see a great need for computer labs. Since students typically have their own computers, we merely need to provide the networking technology so they can access all of the materials they need from wherever they are working. Indeed, every student now has access to every electronic subscription we have through the university's proxy server, and regardless of whether they are in South Carolina or North Carolina, they can access any of the library's resources, including our online catalog, twenty-four hours a day.

Our library now has a fully integrated online system. We purchase MARC records from various venders, and these records are then loaded into our integrated library system. The MARC records include records for materials found on Westlaw, Lexis, and other electronic resources subscribed to or owned by the library. If a student does a search for a law review article and it is found on Westlaw or Lexis, our system will automatically link them to that article.

We are able to give our students access to our materials in several different ways. They can walk into the library and use the online catalog to look up material or ask the reference librarian to assist them, or they can access our online catalog from wherever they may be through our proxy service, and be instantly linked to the resources that are available online. Undoubtedly, technology has greatly increased the accessibility of materials for our faculty and students, and we are continually working to make our materials available in the format they prefer to use. And we make these materials available to our users not only within the law school, but outside of the law school as well.

Helping Students Transition from School to Law Firm

As a law school, one of our directives is to make sure that when our students graduate, they will be able to enter the real world of "lawyering," and do so effectively and efficiently. Our library supports the law school's directive by doing whatever we can to provide services to prepare our students for the day when they will be licensed practicing attorneys. Indeed, one of the most important roles of a law school librarian lies in helping students make the transition from law student to lawyer.

At our law school, the librarians are active in teaching the first-year legal research and writing course, and we believe it is important to teach research methods in both print and electronic formats, because some firms do not subscribe to online services, or they may subscribe to only limited resources because of the expense, while the remainder of their budget may be used to purchase treatises and practice materials in the area of law in which they specialize.

We follow up our instruction in this area by assisting our students when they work as law clerks in the summer. They know our librarians are available to take their calls and help them with any reference problems they are having. Prior to their going out into the real world as summer clerks, we also offer our students workshops to help walk them through the various research processes they may need to use. These workshops provide a refresher course on the materials students covered in their first-year research class, and we introduce them to any resources that were not covered in that class, while making them aware of the practice materials that are available in a particular area of law. For instance, if they are going to be clerking for an attorney who does primarily domestic law, we make them aware of both the electronic and printed resources they may need to use. A student working for an attorney who does mostly domestic law will need to be aware of the North Carolina treatises on family law, the form book available, and the databases that deal specifically with domestic cases. In addition, the student will need to know where forms and other documents can be found online in both subscription-based and free access databases.

I belong to an area law librarians group whose members are librarians for law firms, rather than academic law libraries, and I was recently asked to speak on the topic of our law school's legal research and writing program. The librarians in the group were happily surprised to discover we still teach our students how to use printed resources. One of their major complaints is that the majority of the students hired as summer clerks do not know how to use a loose-leaf service or other printed materials. As a result, they have to spend several weeks at the beginning of each summer training these students, who thought they could use online resources for all of their research. When you work in a law firm, the client is paying for the research you do. Therefore, you have to be very judicious in the way you use online services. Amazingly, these librarians applauded us for the fact that we continue to teach our students how to use both formats.

Throughout our students' law school career, we hold workshops to help them improve their research skills. In addition, whenever they come into the library for assistance, we reinforce the message that we are always available to help them with a reference question. This holds true for our students as well as our graduates.

Helping Students with Research Difficulties

Teaching is increasingly a primary role of the law school librarian, and when students are having difficulties in the research process, it is important to talk with them to get a real feel for the materials they are looking for, and what issues they are trying to resolve. It is important to determine whether the student understands the issue they are researching, or if they have a good understanding of that area of the law. If they do not—which is frequently the case—we recommend that they read a treatise or a hornbook on the area of law to get some background information so they will have a clearer understanding of what the issue is all about. In many cases, treatises and hornbooks may lead the student to law review articles or cases that have been cited in that area, or to other scholarly materials.

Indeed, one of the primary recommendations I make to students who are having research difficulties is that once they have found the basic information, they should see if there is a law review article that has been written on the subject, because law review articles are often a goldmine of information. They offer an in-depth discussion of an issue, and they are meticulous about giving credit to their sources. However, I also warn students that law reviews are not updated, and therefore they will need to update the information from the time the law review was published.

Another research source I recommend to students is the *American Law Reports* series. These volumes are annotated, and their indexes are easy to use. I will often assist students in finding an *American Law Reports* annotation that gives an overview of the subject they are researching. These annotations also discuss specific areas or issues, cite cases and statutes, and provide information about how the majority and minority of states hold on these issues. *American Law Reports* are often a very good starting point for doing research in an area with which you are not familiar.

If a student is doing research that involves a statutory provision, I will send them to an annotated version of the code. The annotated code will cite to cases that have interpreted the provisions of the code, and to law review articles that have addressed the provision. It is a great starting point for this type of research.

Final Thoughts

I believe law school librarians have to be ever vigilant. They have to be constantly aware of the changes that are taking place in this field, and they have to be able to integrate those changes as smoothly as possible into their existing organization or structure. As a law library director, it is also important to encourage your staff to be constantly aware of the changes that are going on within their specific areas, and to encourage them to be involved in professional development so they are constantly being educated with respect to the changes that are taking place. Simply put, you need to make sure you stay on top of the changes in this field, and that your staff is aware of them as well, and then you need to seamlessly put them into place within your existing structure.

Indeed, as a law school librarian, you must constantly strive to educate yourself. Being a librarian is a learning experience. There is never a day that goes by in which I do not learn something new, and I sincerely hope I impart new knowledge to my students as well.

Olivia Leigh Weeks is the director of the Campbell University Norman Adrian Wiggins School of Law and a professor of law. She was licensed to practice law in North Carolina in 1991.

Ms. Weeks earned her B.A. from Meredith College, her M.L.S. from East Carolina University, and her J.D. from the Campbell University School of Law. She is a member of the American Association of Law Libraries, the American Bar Association, and the National Cooperative Business Association.

Dedication: *This chapter is dedicated to the members of the Norman Adrian Wiggins School of Law library staff, who have supported and inspired me over the years.*

Appendices

CONTENTS

APPENDIX A

VISION OF THE COMMUNAL ROLES OF LIBRARIES

The library is a place where knowledge and information freely dwell to define, empower, preserve, challenge, connect, entertain and transform individuals, cultures and communities. The dwelling place, whether physical or virtual, is the product of collective reflection, aspiration, commitment, expertise and organization. It is both a byproduct of civil communities and a catalyst for cultural progress, inspiration, expression and exchange. Its absence in this new century would not only deprive many individuals of important resources, but also, more significantly, such loss would deny humanity an essential portion of its shared identity and entitled liberties. The library can never be fully replaced by information technologies. For the essence of its communal role is not the technological mastery over knowledge and information, but rather the provision of sanctuary for human thought and expression in any medium.

Endorsed the 31st day March, 2005
by Faculty, Fellows and Observers of the Salzburg Seminar,
Libraries in the 21st Century, hosted Oct. 23-30, 2004,
Schloss Leopoldskron, Salzburg, Austria:

Kay Raseroka, Chair Salzburg Session Working Group *Libraries and Their Communities*, International Federation of Library Associations, University of Botswana, Gaborone	Abena Ntrakwah, Ghana International School, Ghana
Yaqub Ali, Islamic Research Institute, International Islamic University, Pakistan	Joan Osborne, Heritage Library Division, National Library and Information Systems Authority, Trinidad and Tobago
Alberta Arthurs, Consultant and Commentator in Arts and Humanities, USA	Pimrumpai Pemsmit, Department of Library Science, Chulalongkorn University, Thailand
Dona Bible, Carnegie-Vincent Library, Lincoln Memorial University, USA	Carol Priestley, International Network for the Availability of Scientific Publications, Oxford University, United Kingdom
Mohammad Hossein Biglu,	Susann Rutledge, BusinessWeek Library, USA
	Renate Schönmayr, Library of the

Department of Library Science, Humbolt University, Germany Paul Callister, Leon E. Block Law Library, University of Missouri-Kansas City School of Law, USA Patrick Craig, Qatar Foundation, Qatar Academy, USA Lourdes David, Rizal Library, Ateneo de Manila University, Philippines Nóra Deák, School of English and American Studies Library, Eötvös Loránd University, Hungary Barbara Doyle-Wilch, Middlebury College, USA Samuel Eyitayo, Information Resource Center, US Consulate General, Lagos Lu-Ann Farrar, Lexington Herald Leader, USA Susan Fifer Canby, National Geographic Society, USA Martín Gómez, Urban Libraries Council, USA Lara Ingham, The Wheeler School, USA Constantin Ittu, Brukenthal Library, Brukenthal Museum, Romania Anthi Katsirikou, Board of the Greek Librarians Association, University of Piraeus, Greece Jocelyn Ladlad, European Documentation and Research Center, American Studies Resource Center, De La Salle University, Philippines Laksmi, Library and Research

Faculty of Law, University of Salzburg, Austria Lillian Sciberras, Division of Library and Information Studies, University of Malta, Malta Thomas Scott, Young Library, Kentucky Christian University, USA Barbara Semonche, Park Library, School of Journalism and Mass Communication, University of North Carolina at Chapel Hill, USA Maqsood Ahmad Shaheen, Information Resource Center, American Embassy, Pakistan Donald Smeeton, William G. Squires Library, Lee University/Church of God Theological Seminary, USA Nadiya Strishenets, Department of United Nations Publication, V. Vernadsky National Library of Ukraine, Ukraine Gordana Stokic, Library and Information Science Department, Faculty of Philology, University of Belgrade, Serbia and Montenegro Ivanka Stricevic, Children and Youth Departments, Medvescak Public Library, Croatia Tirong arap Tanui, Moi University, Kenya Senka Tomljanovic, University Library Rijeka, Croatia Susan Teoh, Information Services Division, Institute of Strategic and International Studies, Malaysia, Kuala Lumpur

Department, Aksara Foundation, Indonesia	Leon Tiemensma, Midrand Graduate Institute, University of South Africa, South Africa
Yuk-Man Lee, Hong Kong Public Libraries, China	Radovan Vrana, Department of Information Sciences, Faculty of Philosophy, University of Zagreb, Croatia
Filiz Ekingen Flores Mamondi, Bogazici University Library, Turkey	
Robert McCutcheon, English Department, Davis and Elkins College, USA	Yiu Chuen Wan, University of Hong Kong Libraries, China
Robert Moropa, Academic Information Service, University of Pretoria, South Africa	Sohair Wastawy, Library of Alexandria, Egypt
Yvonne Murphy, Northern Ireland Political Collection, Linen Hall Library, Northern Ireland	Joan Williams, Thomas F. Holgate Library, Bennett College for Women, USA
Joseph Nga, Collection Management Division, Library of Congress, USA	Yustinus Yuniarto, Tirta Marta-PBK Penabur Christian School, Indonesia
	Liu Zhenxi, Chinese Academy of Social Sciences Library, China

Courtesy of Paul D. Callister, University of Missouri-Kansas City School of Law

APPENDIX B

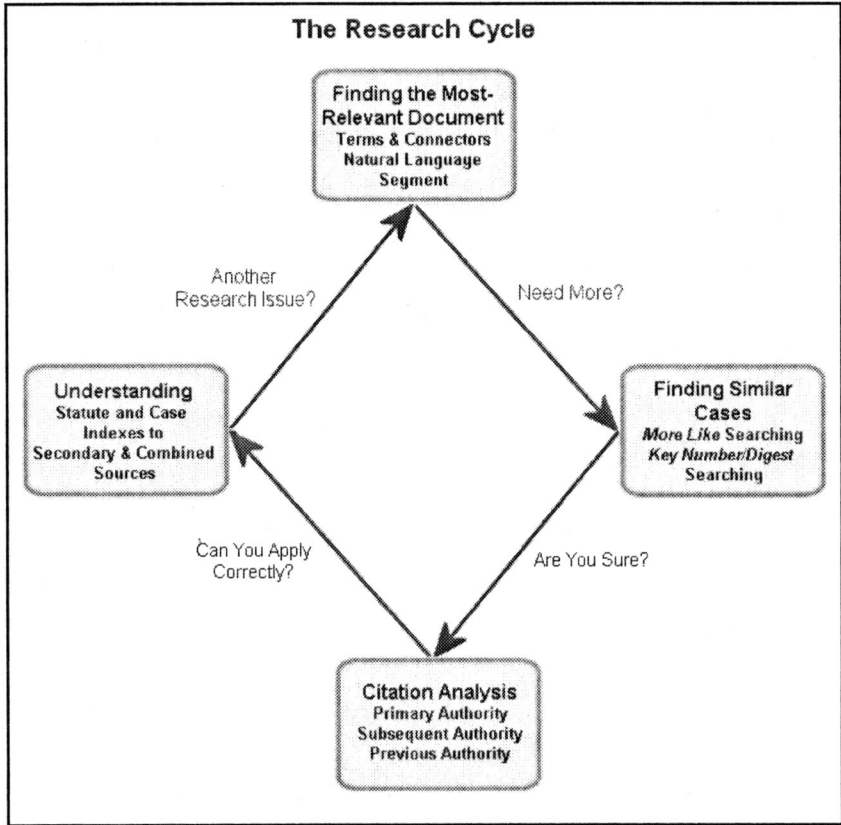

©2004, Paul D. Callister. Image is subject to license terms of the CreativeCommons.org requiring noncommercial use, attribution, and sharing of derivative works under similar terms. See http://creativecommons.org/licenses/by-nc-sa/3.0/us/.

Courtesy of Paul D. Callister, University of Missouri-Kansas City School of Law

APPENDIX C

SECONDARY LAB HANDOUT

Finding Secondary Sources
Library Catalogs and Print Indexes
Law Review Index and Full Text Databases

Part 1 – Why Secondary Sources
Lawyers often start with a secondary source.

- Easier to read and understand
- Well organized
- Contains cites to primary materials
- Leads you to leading cases

> **Today's Research Goal: To find some good lawyer jokes.**

Part 2 – Finding Books
Use catalogs to find books.
Finding Books – *QUEST* – limit my universe to Law Library
    Use keyword searching first, to find a few likely candidates.
        [lawyer jokes]
    Expand search by using identified Library of Congress Subject
    Headings links to see some of what is out there.
        [Lawyers—United States—Humor]
    Advanced search that uses field searching
        [subject keywords: law or lawyer and humor]

Research Challenge:
    Find titles of books in the law library that might contain funny jokes about lawyers.

Part 3 – Locating Law Review Articles with Known Citations

If you have a citation, you may still need to locate the article itself so you can read it.

Finding full text on Westlaw or Lexis only works for those articles online. Virtually no law reviews are on Lexis or Westlaw before 1982, and extensive holdings of law review articles don't start until late 1990s.

Law review volumes at B.C.L.L. The pre-1980 law reviews are in the compact stacks, 1990 to latest bound volume are in stationary stacks, and the latest issues are at Information Desk.

Hein Online for selected older law reviews. [BC access by subscription.]

[18 *Green Bag* 376]

Part 4 – Finding Law Review Articles Using Print Indexes

Subject headings use controlled vocabulary to describe the content of what is being indexed, grouping articles on the same topic (however defined) together.

Print research methodology – Find the correct subject heading and then any articles in the volumes or pamphlets that cover the time you are interested in searching.

The two major general law review indexes:

Index to Legal Periodicals and Books (back to 1920s in print, 1980s electronic)

Theory of indexing – Broad – "User prefers to skim through overly inclusive lists so as not to miss anything."

Current Law Index (back to 1980s print or electronic)

Theory of indexing – Specific – "User wants to go directly to the subject being researched."

Part 5 – Finding Law Review Articles Using Electronic Indexes

Electronic research methodology – Use computer searching power to conduct a key word search; examine your results; and conduct a new, more-focused search using focusing power of controlled vocabulary.

Same two indexes available in a variety of electronic formats – see *Using Law Reviews*.

ILP and LRI databases

Research Challenge:
Use lawyer and joke to find controlled vocabulary for chosen index.

Part 6 – Finding Law Review Articles Using Full Text Searching
Search Methodology – Attempt to predict the words that will be used in a document.
Most comprehensive full-text databases
   Lexis: Law Reviews, Legal Publications Groups File
   Westlaw: TP-ALL

Research Challenge:
Find funny articles or articles with lawyer jokes in them by predicting the words that will be used in a funny article.

Part 7 – General Hints for Finding Secondary Sources Effectively
See hints in *Using Law Reviews*
Compare index access with full text access
   You can only find what is there. Know the scope of the index or full-
      text database – specific content and years of coverage for each
      journal.
   Articles are indexed on major topics of discussion but, full-text
      searching can also bring up tangential discussions.
   Choose your words carefully. In full-text searching, think of words that
      will be used in the discussion itself, in index searching, browse the
      subjects list or examine the subject headings of an easy to find
      entry to find the words that will be used to describe the subject.

Courtesy of Joan Shear, Boston College Law Library

APPENDIX D

CHECKLIST FOR LEGISLATIVE HISTORY HANDOUT

_____ **A.   Obtain the Public Law Number and Statutes at Large Number for the Legislation**

_____   1.   Recently Passed Legislation

(a)   Congressional Index
_____   Recent Bill
_____   Know Subject of the Bill but not the Popular Name
_____   Gives the Public Law Number, Statutes at Large Cite

(b)   Shepard's Acts and Cases by Popular Names
_____   know the name of the Act
_____   Gives the Public Law Number, Statutes at Large Number, and U.S.C. cite

_____   2.   If the Legislation has been codified and you have the cite to the U.S.C., you use the following steps to find the P.L. number and the Statutes at Large cite.

(a)   U.S.C. and U.S.C.S.
_____   Find the Statute in the U.S.C.
_____   Go to the end of the code section.
_____   You will be given the Public Law Number and the Statutes at Large cite

(b)   U.S.C.A.
_____   Find the Statute in the U.S.C.A.
_____   At the end of the code section, you will be given the date of enactment, the public law number, and the Statutes at Large cite.
_____   Find the "Historical and Statutory Notes," and look for the sub-topic "Legislative History."
_____   If there is a legislative history reference, you will be given the cite to the legislative history in the U.S.C.C.A.N.

_____ **B.   Compiled Legislative Histories**

_____ 1.   Determine if a legislative history has been compiled by someone else. Check the public catalog or a publication which references compiled legislative histories. If you are lucky enough to locate a compiled legislative history, a major part of your task has been done.

_____ 2.   Compiled Legislative Histories are indexed in three excellent sources

Sources of Compiled Legislative History - Johnson
Sources of Compiled Legislative History - looseleaf service with coverage from the first Congress to the present
Union List of Legislative Histories - 1881 to present

_____ **C.   Compiling Your Own Legislative History**

_____ 1.   If there isn't a compiled legislative history, then you must find a list of the documents which make up the legislative history for the bill, and then locate the actual documents. The best starting point for this exercise is the United States Code Congressional and Administrative News.

_____ 2.   United States Code Congressional and Administrative News

This is a series of books published by Thomson West
It is indispensable in keeping abreast of current federal legislative documents and is an excellent source for locating earlier legislative histories
The purpose of this series is to supply in one place verbatim copies of federal legislative materials less easily found in official form
It is issued semimonthly during each session of Congress in the form of   advance sheets, and the annual volumes covering a session are bound.

_____ 3.   U.S.C.C.A.N. Approach

(a)   Compiling the History
_____   Obtain the Public Law Number and/or Statutes at Large number
         for the Act
_____   Pull the USCCAN volume which contains the Public Law Number
         for the Act you are researching
_____   Turn to the page on which your Public Law Begins

         the Public Law number appears in the upper right-hand corner of
         the page
         the Statutes at large number appears at the bottom of the page

_____   The Bill as enacted begins on this page; the publication gives some
         notes in the margin
_____   On the first page under the name of the act, you will be told where
         the Legislative History for the act is located.
_____   Go to the volume and page given for the Legislative History.
_____   On the first page of the Legislative History, you are given a
         complete list of the documents which make up the legislative
         history.

         date the statute was enacted
         Statutes at Large Citation
         Committee Report Numbers for House and Senate
         Names of the Committees Reporting on the bill
         Congressional Record Volume and dates when the house and
         senate considered the bill

(b)   Locating the Documents
_____   Some, but not all, of the documents are reprinted in the
         U.S.C.C.A.N.
_____   Full text of the Public Laws are reprinted in the volumes labeled
         "Laws."
_____   House or Senate Committee Reports are reprinted in the volumes
         labeled "Legislative History."
_____   Conference Committee Reports are reprinted in the "Legislative
         History" volume for the bill.
_____   Presidential Signing Statement is found at the end of the Legislative
         History for the bill.

Note:

_____ The bill in its original form can be found in the Congressional Record

_____ The Senate and/or House debates can also be found in the Congressional Record

_____ 4.   Statutes at Large Approach

_____ Take the Statutes at Large cite.

_____ Find the volume of the Statues at Large which contains the document you need.

_____ If the volume is 88 or lower, there will be a Table in the back entitled "Guide to Legislative History of Bills Enacted into Public Law"

_____ Look up the Public Law Number on the table, and it will list references to the legislative documents for the Public Law

_____ If the volume is 89 or higher, the legislative history is printed with the statute

_____ **D.   Locating Documents Not Housed in the Law Library**

_____ 1.   Government Depository Libraries

_____ If the documents you need aren't located in the law library, go to the nearest Government Documents Library.

_____ Carrie Rich Memorial Library , the undergrad library, is a selective Government Depository Library which houses many government documents.

_____ Tell the librarian what you need, and she will find it for you.

_____ 2.   Internet Access to Federal Documents (Non-Subscription Based)

_____ If you don't want to go to the Undergrad Library to look for information, you can always "surf the net." There are several web sites which give access to many of the documents needed to compile a legislative history.

_____ University of Michigan Documents Center

_____ http://www.lib.umich.edu/govdocs/
Legislative Process
Bill Indexes
Congressional Research Service Reports
Bill Texts and Status
Published and Unpublished Hearings
Reports and Documents
Floor Debates in the Congressional Record

_____ Internet law Library
http://www.lectlaw.com/inll/1.htm
Chose the option for U.S. Federal Laws (by original published source)
Chose the option for the Congressional Record, Hearings of Congressional committees, or House and Senate Documents.

_____ United States Government Printing Office
http://www.access.gpo.gov/

_____ Thomas - legislative Information on the Internet
http://thomas.loc.gov/
Congress this week
Bills (101st and 107th Congress)
Congressional Record (101st - 107th Congress)
Committee Information (104th - 107th Congress)
Historical Documents
Legislative Process

_____ North Carollina Legislative Library
http://www.ncga.state.nc.us/LegLibrary/
Click on link to Research Guide.
Click on Link to Compiling a Legislative History

_____ 3.   Internet Access to Federal Resources (Subscription Based)

_____ Westlaw
www.lawschool.westlaw.com
Database : USCCAN
Public Laws
All Congressional Committee Reports (1990 - present)
Legislative Histories 1948 - present)
Presidential Proclamations
Executive Orders

_____ Lexis
http://www.lexisnexis.com/lawschool/
Bill Text & Tracking
Legislative Histories
Congressional Record Materials

_____ CIS (Congressional Index Service)
http://web.lexis nexis.com/congcomp
Reports
House and Senate Documents
Committee Prints
Bills
Congressional Record
Testimony in Congressional Hearings
Bill Tracking
Legislative Histories

Proper Citation Form for Legislative Materials

A.   BILLS

1.   Unenacted Federal Bills

Rule 13.2

International Dolphin Conservation Program Act, H.R. 408, 105th Cong. 3 (1997).

1.	If relevant, include the name of the bill in regular type.	
2.	Give the abbreviated name for the house	
	a.	H.R. = House of Representatives
	b.	S. = Senate
3.	Give the number of the bill	
4.	Give the Congress (abbreviate Congress = Cong.)	

Note: Unless the documents were published in the late 1800's or early 1900's, you do not give the session of Congress. (Rule 13)

5.	Give the of any
6.	Give the year of publication

Rule 13.2(a)

2.   Enacted Federal Bills

1.	General Rule - cite as Statutes

Rule 13.2(b)

Rule 12

2.	Exception - if the bill is used to document Legislative History, cite as an unenacted bill.

Rule 13.2(b)

B.   HEARINGS

Rule 13.3

Reduction in Dolphin Mortality: Hearings on H.R. 408 Before the Comm. On Resources, 105th Cong. 25 (1997) (statement of Paul N. Van der Water, Assistant Director for Budget Analysis).

1. Give the title as it appears on the cover of the Report. Underscore or italicize the title.
   a. Include the bill number
   b. Give the subcommittee and/or committee name which conducted the hearings
2. Give the Congress
3. Give the page number for the materials being cited
4. Year of publication
5. If you are citing a specific statement, indicate the information in parenthesis.
   a. Give the speaker's full name
   b. Give the speaker's title

Rule 13.3

C.   REPORTS

Rule 13.4

S. Rep. No. 105-52, at 1 (1997).

1. Give the Name of the House
   a. H.R. Rep. = House of Representatives Report
   b. S. Rep. = Senate Report
   c. H.R. Conf. Rep. = House of Representatives Conference Report
   d. S. Conf. Rep. = Senate Conference Report
2. Give the number of the Congress and the Report number. Separate the two numbers with a hyphen.

3. Give the page number on which the material appears preceded by the word "at."
4. Give the year of publication.

H.R. Rep. No. 105-74, at 7 (1997), reprinted in 1997 U.S.C.C.A.N. 1628.

1. For documents published after 1974, give a parallel cite to the United States Code and Congressional News
2. Give the name of the house, the number of the Congress and Report Number, the page number, and the year of publication.
3. Indicate the report is a reprint by preceding the USCCAN cite with the words "reprinted in." "Reprinted in" is either underscored (use a continuing line for the phrase) or italicized.
4. Give the year of the USCCAN volume, U.S.C.C.A.N., and the beginning page number of the report.

D.   DEBATES

Rule 13.5

144 Cong. Rec. S9550 (daily ed. July 31, 1998) (statement of Sen. Kennedy).

1. Cite Congressional Debates to the Congressional Record.
2. Cite to the daily edition only if the debates do not yet appear in the bound edition.
3. Give the volume number of the Congressional Record, Indicate it is the Cong. Rec. you are citing, and give the page number on which the statement appears. If you are citing to the daily edition, you must indicate whether the page is in the House or Senate section of the issue.
4. Give the date of the issue (month, day, year)
5. If you are citing to a specific statement, give the information in parenthesis.

144 Cong. Rec. 18,800 (1998)

1. Cite to the bound volume if available
2. Give the volume number and the page in the bound volume. In the bound volume, there is no separate pagination for the House or Senate; therefore, the page number will not require a prefix.
3. Give the year of publication

Courtesy of Olivia Leigh Weeks, Campbell University Norman Adrian Wiggins School of Law

APPENDIX E

HEALTH CARE DIRECTIVES HANDOUT

INTRODUCTION

We all plan for today B but have you planned for tomorrow? Whether your assets are great or small, the law gives you the right to say who will manage your estate after your death. The law also gives you the right to decide how your estate will be distributed. You can assert these rights by making a will. Without a will, this decision will be made in accordance with North Carolina Law, and quite often, what the law dictates is not what you would have wanted or what is best for the estate and the beneficiaries.

You should have a will; however, planning for the future encompasses more than having an attorney draft your will. What happens if you suddenly become ill and you are unable to take care of your affairs? Who will manage your banking and business affairs? Your family can ask the court to appoint a guardian to make business decisions for you, but wouldn't you rather choose who manages your affairs in the event of a crisis?

What about health care decisions? Who will make these decisions for you if you are unable to make them yourself? How can you make sure your wishes regarding healthcare will be carried out?

There are several documents which provide for continuity of supervision for a person's estate in times of temporary or permanent illness, absence, or incapacity. In addition, there are health care directives which can be made by an individual before an illness or incapacity strikes; decisions which make it much easier for loved ones to carry out an individual's wishes at a time and under circumstances which are least conducive to making life and death decisions.

This guide explains a few of the documents which can be used to insure continuity of supervision for an estate. It also includes medical directives which can be used to notify doctors of one's wishes regarding healthcare.

In addition, sample forms which meet the statutory requirements set forth in the North Carolina General Statutes are included in this guide. Attached are sample forms for a General Power of Attorney, a Durable Power of Attorney, a Healthcare Power of Attorney, and a Living Will.

WILLS

INTRODUCTION

Planning is about the future. Estate planning is about your future. When the word "estate" is used, most people picture a twenty room mansion on a 10 acre parcel of land. The word "estate," however, simply means all the property a person owns. This includes personal property (cars, clothing, jewelry, etc.), real property (home or land), as well as any financial assets (bank accounts, investments, etc.).

A will is a legal document by which a person (testator or testatrix) makes a disposition of his or her estate. The effect of a will takes place after death; therefore, the will can be changed at anytime during the lifetime of the testator or testatrix. It can also be revoked at anytime during the testator's/testatrix's lifetime.

A properly drawn will should make the administration of an estate simpler. Most of us have avoided making a will because we are unwilling to face the question of our death. But remember, a will is simply a legal document which sets forth clearly and legally the manner in which you want your property distributed following your death.

SHOULD YOU HAVE A WILL?

If the following things are important to you, you need a will.

You wish to avoid intestacy laws.

When a person dies without a Will or dies "intestate," the property of the deceased is distributed according to a formula fixed by law. Therefore, if you don't make a will, you do not have any say as to how your property will be distributed.

You want to minimize taxes.

A properly drafted Will may reduce the amount of taxes that have to be paid. Wills drafted without consideration of recent federal and North Carolina tax laws should be re-examined.

You want to direct the distribution of your property.

Most property may be distributed in any way a person wishes. There are a few exceptions to this rule. For example, a husband or wife cannot completely exclude his or her spouse. Also, some property may be controlled by other provisions of the law and not by the Will. For example, joint bank accounts and real property held in the names of both a husband and wife usually pass to the survivor by law and not by the terms of the will. Additional proceeds which may be controlled by other provisions of law are insurance proceeds, jointly owned property, and retirement benefits.

You want to develop a long-range plan of financial care for a son or daughter who is disabled.

You want to establish a trust under your Will.

IMPORTANCE OF A WILL

A Will distributes your property according to your wishes at your death.

A Will names a person of your choosing who will make certain the directions of your Will are followed. This person is called either an Executor (man) or Executrix (woman).

A Will gives instructions for the payment of debt, taxes, burial expenses, etc.

FORMALITIES OF MAKING A WILL

WHO MAY MAKE A WILL?

A person must be a least 18 years of age to make a Will.

In addition, the person must be of sound mind, and he or she must be free from improper influence by another person.

HOW DOES ONE MAKE A WILL?

A Will should be written, witnessed by two competent witnesses, and signed by the testator (person making the Will) in strict accordance with North Carolina law.

The testator (man) or testatrix (woman) must sign the Will prior to the attestation by the witnesses. An attesting witness is one who signs his or her name to the Will for the purpose of proving and identifying the document. In North Carolina, the law requires that the attesting witnesses sign the Will in the presence of the testator or testatrix.

The witnesses to the Will should not be a beneficiary under the Will or the husband or wife of a beneficiary under the Will.

The signature of the testator or testatrix and the witnesses' signatures should be certified by a Notary Public.

CAN A WILL BE CHANGED?

Until your death, your Will is not permanent. It can be changed as often as you desire.

Changes can be made by either drafting a new Will or by the addition of a amendment called a codicil.

Any change or codicil to the Will must comply with the same laws that apply to the making of a Will.

HOW LONG IS A WILL VALID?

A Will which is properly written and executed remains valid until it is changed or revoked.

However, changes in circumstances after a Will is made can affect the adequacy of the Will or change the manner in which the estate will be distributed. Some of the changes which can affect the Will are marriage, divorce, the birth of a child, or a change in the nature or amount of the person's estate.

When there is a change in circumstances, an individual should review all the provisions of his or her current Will and change the Will to conform to the new situation.

Each person should review his or her Will at least every five years to make sure the provisions in the Will are still appropriate.

POWER OF ATTORNEY

INTRODUCTION

Who will manage your banking and business affairs if a sudden illness or accident leaves you incapacitated? Your family can ask the court to appoint a guardian to make decisions for you, but don't you want to choose the person who will manage your affairs in the event of a crisis?

A power of attorney is a document in which you give someone the legal authority to act for you. That person is called your attorney-in-fact or your agent. You are called the principal. You may name your spouse, an adult child, a relative, or a trusted friend to be your agent. You should choose someone you trust completely. The actions of your attorney-in-fact authorized by your power of attorney are considered legally to be your actions.

A power of attorney can give either broad or limited powers to the attorney-in-fact. A power of attorney can also be designed to survive the incapacity or mental incompetence of the principal.

TYPES OF POWERS OF ATTORNEY

There are two types of powers of attorney B a durable power of attorney and a general power of attorney.

DURABLE POWER OF ATTORNEY

A durable power of attorney is effective even if the principal is incapacitated. Therefore, if you are planning for possible future incompetency, your power of attorney must be durable. To be durable, a power of attorney must state that it either remains or becomes effective after you have become incapacitated, or it must refer to Article 2 of Chapter 32A of the North Carolina General Statutes.

GENERAL POWER OF ATTORNEY

A general power of attorney ends if the principal becomes incompetent or incapacitated. Someone may act on your behalf under a regular power of attorney only if you are competent. Therefore, a regular power of attorney is used for reasons other than planning for incapacity.

POWERS GRANTED TO THE ATTORNEY-IN-FACT UNDER A STATUTORY POWER OF ATTORNEY

The statutory power of attorney in North Carolina grants to the attorney-in-fact powers that are "broad and sweeping."

The statute confers at least the following powers:

- To lease, purchase, exchange, and acquire real property
- To lease, purchase, exchange, and acquire personal property
- To bond, share, and commodity transactions
- To make banking transactions
- To have access to safe deposit boxes and vaults
- To conduct any business operating transactions
- To exercise or perform insurance transactions
- To do all acts necessary for maintaining the customary standard of living of the principal
- To prepare any social security or unemployment insurance documents
- To execute vouchers for military service benefits
- To prepare any and all types of tax returns and documents

- To employ agents such as legal counsel, accountants, or other professionals.

EFFECTIVE DATE AND DURATION

GENERAL POWER OF ATTORNEY

A general power of attorney becomes effective on the date it is executed unless a different date is specified on the form. The principal may give the date the power of attorney goes into effect and the date it terminates on the form.

Unless otherwise indicated, the power of attorney remains effective until (1) the death of the principal, (2) the incapacitation of the principal, (3) the date the power of attorney is revoked by the principal, or (4) the date of termination indicated on the document.

DURABLE POWER OF ATTORNEY

A durable power of attorney can survive the disability or incapacity of the principal. The power is not automatic; there must be specific language in the document to trigger a durable power of attorney.

Also, a durable power of attorney is valid after you become incapacitated only if it is registered in the office of the register of deeds in at least one of the following places:

- The county named in your power of attorney,
- The county of your legal residence,
- The county where you own real property if you have no legal residence in North Carolina), or
- The county where your attorney-in-fact lives.

Note: Your durable power of attorney may be registered by your Attorney-in-Fact after you become incapacitated.

A durable power of attorney may be effective immediately or only if you become incapacitated. A power of attorney that becomes effective only upon the disability or incapacity of the principal is called a "springing" power of attorney. Special language on the document creates this power of attorney.

REVOCATION OF A DURABLE POWER OF ATTORNEY

DURABLE POWER OF ATTORNEY WHICH HASN'T BEEN REGISTERED

If you haven't registered it, it can be revoked in several ways. In any event, your attorney-in-fact should be notified that the power of attorney has been revoked.

Your death revokes your power of attorney.

You may provide a method for revoking it in your power of attorney.

You may destroy the power of attorney if you are competent.

If you are competent, you may revoke your durable power of attorney by a written document that is signed, notarized, and sent to your attorney-in-fact by certified or registered mail.

REGISTERED DURABLE POWER OF ATTORNEY

If you have registered your durable power of attorney, it will be terminated by one of the following events.

Your death revokes your power of attorney.

If you are competent, you make revoke your durable power of attorney by filing a written revocation in the register of deeds office where you filed your power of attorney. You must serve notice of the revocation on your attorney-in-fact.

Your attorney-in-fact dies or resigns, and you haven't named someone else to take his or her place.

POWERS OF ATTORNEY B STATUTORY FORMS

SHORT FORM POWER OF ATTORNEY

GENERALLY

A short form power of attorney may be used in situations where the principal grants only a few powers to the attorney-in-fact.

The short form may be used where the power of attorney is to end on a specific date.

It is generally appropriate to use a short form to create a durable power of attorney that survives the subsequent incapacity or mental incompetence of the principal.

FORMALITIES

The Form must give both the name and address of the principal and the attorney-in-fact.

The principal must initial the line which corresponds to the areas in which the principle desires to give the attorney-in-fact authority to act on his/her behalf.

The principal must sign and date the form in the presence of a Notary.

The signature of the principal must then be notarized.

If a durable power of attorney is created, it must be registered with the register of deeds of the county in which the principal resides, the county names in the power of attorney, or the county in which the attorney-in-fact lives in order for the power of attorney to be valid subsequent to the principal's incapacity or mental incompetence.

LONG FORM POWER OF ATTORNEY

GENERALLY

In many situations, a power of attorney is desirable to provide continuity of supervision for a person's estate in times of temporary or permanent illness, absence or incapacity.

Generally, the statutory long form power of attorney is a broad durable power of attorney designed to authorize the attorney-in-fact to exercise powers relating to the principal's property and to make decisions concerning the principal's personal affairs.

In North Carolina, a durable power of attorney may include a "springing" power-- a provision that the power of attorney is effective only upon the happening of some specified event such as the principal's incapacity.

FORMALITIES

Power of attorney must be in writing. In order for the power of attorney to be durable, it must contain words to the effect that "the power of attorney will not be affected by the subsequent disability or incapacity of the principal or lapse or time" or it must state the power of attorney will become effective upon a specified occurrence.

The document must be signed and dated by the principal in the presence of a notary.

A duly commissioned notary must notarize the document.

The power of attorney should be registered with the register of deeds of the county in which the principal resides, the county named in the power of attorney, or the county where the attorney-in-fact lives. If the power of attorney is not registered, it will not be valid subsequent to the principal's incapacity or mental incompetence.

HEALTH CARE DECISIONS

INTRODUCTION

As an alert, competent adult, you have the right to make decisions concerning your own health care. You can decide to proceed with certain treatments or operations or you can decide not to undergo them. The trouble arises when you are no longer capable of making such decisions.

Medical technology has progressed so far in this country that it's often possible to keep a person alive well beyond the point where that person's life has meaning and quality. In the past, most people had a personal physician who knew what their wishes were concerning life-sustaining measures and, the doctor would be available and able to ensure a peaceful death with dignity. Today, however, many people don't have a personal physician or, if they do, the physician may not be available when needed. For these reasons, it is very important for you to write down your wishes regarding your health care and to appoint someone you trust to make decisions for you when you can't make them for yourself.

You may have heard of a Living Will, a legal document in North Carolina that safeguards your right to determine the kind of care you'll receive at the end of your life. The Living Will is one of several advance care documents by which competent people instruct their family, physicians, friends, lawyers, ministers, and other important people in their lives about their wishes for medical care should they become unable to speak or decide for themselves.

A Health Care Power of Attorney, a legal document in North Carolina. is another advance care document. When you execute a Health Care Power of Attorney you name a person to make your health-related decisions for you when you no longer can.

HEALTH CARE POWER OF ATTORNEY

INTRODUCTION

There is a better chance that your medical care will be handled the way you want if you have a Health Care Power of Attorney.

Simply telling your family what you want done isn't enough. You need to give someone the legal right to make health care decisions for you if you become unable to make these decisions yourself.

WHAT IS A HEALTH CARE POWER OF ATTORNEY?

A health care power of attorney is a document that gives another person the authority to make medical decisions on your behalf.

The person signing the document, the principal, appoints another person as a health care attorney-in-fact.

Choose your health care attorney-in-fact very carefully. He or she will have the right to make life and death decisions on your behalf. Make sure your health care attorney-in-fact understands your wishes and is able to carry them out.

The powers granted to your health care attorney-in-fact are effective only when the physician or physicians designated in the form determine that you are unable to make health care decisions yourself.

You should be aware that the health care power of attorney grants the health care attorney-in-fact the power to authorize the withholding of life-sustaining procedures under certain circumstances and thus the power of attorney may conflict with a Living Will. If you have executed a Living Will, the Living Will controls the decision as to whether and when life-sustaining procedures will be withheld or discontinued.

A health care power of attorney does not require the health care attorney-in-fact to exercise the powers granted to him or her. Therefore, the form enables you to designate successor health care attorneys-in fact in the event the original health care attorney-in-fact is unwilling to act or is unable to act.

WHAT POWERS ARE GRANTED YOUR HEALTH CARE ATTORNEY-IN-FACT UNDER NORTH CAROLINA LAW?

The North Carolina statutory health care power of attorney states that the powers granted to the health care attorney-in-fact are "broad and sweeping."

The statute confers at least the following powers to the health care attorney-in-fact:

- The authority to request, review, and receive medical information;
- The authority to consent to the disclosure of medical and hospital records;
- The authority to employ and discharge health care providers;
- The authority to authorize admission and discharge from hospitals, nursing or convalescent homes, and other institutions;
- The authority to consent to or withdraw consent for diagnostic and treatment procedures;
- The authority to consent to measures for relief of pain;
- The authority to authorize the withholding of or withdrawal of life-sustaining procedures under specific circumstances;
- The authority to make disposition of any part or all of the body for medical purposes, organ donation, or autopsy;
- The authority to take any lawful actions necessary to carry out the health care power of attorney.

Any of the powers in the statutory health care power of attorney can be removed. In addition, similar powers can be included.

CAN YOU HAVE BOTH A HEALTH CARE POWER OF ATTORNEY AND A LIVING WILL?

Yes. You may have a Health Care Power of Attorney which designates an individual to act on your behalf and a Living Will which indicates your choice of health care in the event you are unable to make those decisions in the future.

In fact, you may have a Living Will and a Health Care Power of Attorney in the same document. By addressing these issues in a single document, the risk of any inconsistency in separate documents can be avoided.

HOW DO YOU MAKE A HEALTH CARE POWER OF ATTORNEY?

The forms used to make a Health Care Power of Attorney may be obtained from an attorney.

A Health care power of attorney must be in writing.

The Health Care Power of Attorney must be signed by you in the presence of two qualified witnesses.

A qualified witness is one who is not related to you, will not inherit from your estate, and is not your physician or employed by your physician.

The document is to be notarized by a duly commissioned notary.

A copy of the completed document should be given to the health care attorney-in-fact and any alternate named in the power of attorney, to the attending physician, and members of the family.

WHEN DOES MY HEALTH CARE POWER OF ATTORNEY BECOME EFFECTIVE?

Your health care power of attorney does not become effective immediately.

The document becomes effective when the physician designated in the power of attorney determines that you lack sufficient understanding or capacity to make health care decisions.

REVOCATION

Your Health Care Power of Attorney is revoked at your death.

Your Health Care Power of Attorney may be revoked by you at any time by executing and acknowledging an instrument of revocation or a subsequent health care power of attorney or in any other manner communicating the intent to revoke.

The revocation will become effective only upon communication by you to each health care attorney-in-fact named in the Health Care Power of Attorney and to your attending physician.

DECLARATION OF A DESIRE FOR A NATURAL DEATH LIVING WILL

WHAT IS A LIVING WILL?

In North Carolina, a Living Will is called a "Declaration of Desire for a Natural Death."

A Living Will is a document which allows you to retain control over whether your life will be prolonged by certain medical procedures if you are diagnosed terminally ill or in a persistent vegetative state.

The attending physician plus a second physician must confirm your condition before the terms of your Living Will can be honored.

Signing the form and subsequent actions under the Living Will are not considered suicide. Similarly, the physician or medical facility personnel who act as prescribed are protected from civil or criminal liability.

WHAT ARE THE REQUIREMENTS FOR MAKING A LIVING WILL?

You must be at least 18 years of age and of sound mind when you sign your Living Will.

You must express your desire that you do not want your doctor to use extraordinary means or artificial nutrition or hydration to keep you alive if your condition is terminal and incurable or if you are in a persistent vegetative state.

You must state that you know your living will allows your doctor to withhold or stop extraordinary medical treatment or artificial nutrition or hydration.

WHAT ARE YOUR OPTIONS IN A LIVING WILL?

You must instruct the doctor what you want done if your condition is terminal and incurable or if you are in a persistent vegetative state. You may make choices by initialing the appropriate options. If you make no choices, your Living Will is meaningless. If you make inconsistent choices, your Living Will is confusing and may not accomplish what you want.

Read the choices carefully before initialing them to make sure that your intentions are clear.

If your condition is terminal and incurable, your living will may instruct your doctor to do the following:

- to withhold or stop extraordinary means only, or
- to withhold or stop both extraordinary means and artificial nutrition or hydration.

If you are in a persistent vegetative state, your Living Will may instruct your doctor to do the following:

- to withhold or stop extraordinary means only, or
- to withhold or stop both extraordinary means and artificial nutrition or hydration.

EXECUTING A LIVING WILL

You must be of sound mind to execute the "Declaration of a Desire for a Natural Death."

The Living Will must be signed by you in the presence of two qualified witnesses.

Qualified witnesses are witnesses who do not have a special interest in your death such as your relatives.

A notary public must certify your Living Will.

Your Living Will should be kept in a readily accessible location. You should make your immediate family and your physician aware of the declaration.

WHAT IS THE EFFECT OF A LIVING WILL?

Your Living Will gives your doctor permission to withhold or discontinue life support systems under two conditions.

- You must be terminally and incurably ill, or
- You must be diagnosed as being in a persistent vegetative state.

If two doctors diagnose one of these conditions, your doctor may withhold or discontinue extraordinary medical treatment as directed by your Living Will.

HOW CAN YOU REVOKE YOUR LIVING WILL?

You may revoke your Living Will by communicating your desire to your doctor.

You may use any means available to communicate your intent to revoke.

Your mental or physical condition isn't considered, so you do not need to be of sound mind.

Someone acting on your behalf may also tell your doctor that you want to revoke your Living Will.

Revocation is effective only after your doctor has been notified.

If you sign a new Living Will, be sure to revoke all prior Living Wills that may be inconsistent with your new Living Will.

DO NOT RESUSCITATE (DNR) ORDERS

WHAT IS A DNR ORDER AND HOW IS IT MADE?

A DNR order is issued by a patient's doctor stating that if the patient's heart should stop beating, or if the patient should stop breathing, no effort should be made to resuscitate him or her.

Ordinarily, a doctor writes a DNR order for patients who are terminally and incurably ill, or in a persistent vegetative state, and who do not want their life needlessly prolonged by resuscitation efforts.

HOW DOES A DNR ORDER DIFFER FROM A LIVING WILL?

A Living Will is a patient's decision not to have his or her life prolonged by artificial means when there is no reasonable hope for recovery. A Living Will allows you to make this decision in advance.

A DNR order is a medical order issued by a patient's doctor after it has been determined that the patient is dying or in a persistent vegetative state. A DNR order is entered after the doctors have determined that a patient's Living Will should be honored.

However, a patient doesn't need to have a Living Will before a DNR order can be entered.

A Living Will and a DNR order are different documents that can work together, but one isn't dependent on the other.

WHAT HAPPENS IF YOU HAVE A DNR ORDER?

A DNR order should be kept with the patient. If the patient is at home or in a nursing home, and his or her heart stops beating or he or she stops breathing, the DNR order will tell Emergency Medical Services (EMS) who are called not to resuscitate the patient.

If the patient has a DNR order, EMS should not be called. However, family members sometimes panic and call for help when they see their loved one in distress. The DNR order helps make sure the patient's wishes are honored.

WHAT HAPPENS IF YOU DON'T HAVE A DNR ORDER?

If you heart stops beating or you stop breathing and EMS is called, they will resuscitate you if you do not have a DNR order.

It is the duty of EMS to resuscitate patients whom they are called to help. Unless the patient has a DNR order, EMS must try to resuscitate the patient.

ON-LINE CENTRAL REGISTRY FOR ADVANCE DIRECTIVES

WHAT IS THE ON-LINE CENTRAL REGISTRY?

North Carolina has provided a way for your advance directives to be registered in a central location so your documents are available to the appropriate people when they are needed.

Beginning July 2002, you can register your advance directives with the Secretary of State's Office to make them available from a central database 24 hours a day, 7 days a week.

WHAT ADVANCE DIRECTIVES CAN BE REGISTERED?

Health Care Power of Attorney

A Declaration of a Desire for a Natural Death B Living Will

An Advance Instruction for Mental Health Treatment

A Declaration of an Anatomical Gift.

HOW DO YOU REGISTER YOUR ADVANCE DIRECTIVES WITH THE ON-LINE CENTRAL REGISTRY?

You must mail the original document to the Secretary of State's Office.

Only the person who executed the documents may submit them for registration.

If you want to register your documents, you must do so while you are still competent because your authorized attorney-in-fact can't register them for you.

Each document must be notarized.

Your Living Will, health care power of attorney, and advance instruction for mental health treatment should be notarized when you sign them.

A donor card isn't usually notarized; therefore, you must remember to have it notarized before you register it.

A Filing fee of $10.00 must be paid for each document submitted.

You must give a return address so the original documents can be returned to you.

WHAT HAPPENS AFTER YOU REGISTER YOUR ADVANCE DIRECTIVES?

The Secretary of State's Office creates a digital reproduction of each document and enters it into the registry database.

The Secretary of State's Office returns the original document to you along with a wallet sized card that contains a unique file number and password for that document. You must be careful not to lose the file number and password provided on the wallet card.

WHO HAS ACCESS TO YOUR ADVANCE DIRECTIVES?

Each document is accessible over the Internet, 24 hours a day and 7 days a week, to people who have the file number and password. People who have access will be able to look at the documents and print a copy of them. They will not be able to delete or modify the documents in the registry database.

You control who has access by giving the file number and password to the people of your choice.

Your health care providers and your health care attorney-in-fact should have the file number and password for each advance directive, so they can access the documents when necessary.

Also consider giving the file number and password to selected family members who will be able to remind your health care providers that you have an advance directive. Your family members can help see that your choices are respected, but they must first know what your choices are.

HOW DO YOU REMOVE A DOCUMENT FROM THE REGISTRY?

To remove a document from the registry database, you must file a revocation.

A revocation merely removes the document from the database   it does not revoke the document.

To remove a document from the registry database, you should file a written, notarized revocation with the Secretary of State's Office.

The revocation must contain the document's file number and password.

There is no fee to file a revocation.

Removing an advance directive from the registry database does not revoke the advance directive. To revoke the advance directive, you must follow the rules for revoking that particular type of advance directive.

If you have followed the rules and revoked your advance directive, it is revoked even if you do not remove it from the registry database. However, if you do not remove a revoked advance directive from the registry database, you risk having it honored even though you have changed your mind.

So, remember to remove any outdated or revoked versions of your advance directives from the database.

HOW DO YOU REPLACE A DOCUMENT IN THE REGISTRY?

Suppose you amend an advance directive. For example, you may want to name a new health care agent. Currently, there is no provision for replacing the old version with a new version and keeping the same file number and password.

If you update an advance directive that is registered with the Secretary of State, you need to follow these steps.

Register the updated version with the Secretary of State's Office as a new document and get a new file number and password.

File a revocation to remove the old version from the database. (Also, check with your attorney to make sure that you have legally revoked the old version.)

Update your medical files with the new file number and password, and give the new information to your health care agent and selected family members.

Courtesy of Olivia Leigh Weeks, Campbell University Norman Adrian Wiggins School of Law

APPENDIX F

HOW TO LOCATE U.S. SUPREME COURT CASES AND RELATED MATERIALS HANDOUT

Basic Structure of the United States Court System

United States Supreme Court
Published Decisions
U.S. Reports (official)
Supreme Court Reporter
Lawyer's Edition

North Carolina Supreme Court
Published Decisions
N.C. Reports (official)
Southeastern Reporter
Southeastern Reporter

United States Court of Appeals
Published Decisions
Federal Reporter
Federal Reporter 2d
Federal Reporter 3d
Southeastern Reporter

North Carolina Court of Appeals
Published Decisions
N.C. Court of Appeals
Reports
Southeastern Reporter

United States District Courts
Published Decisions
Federal Supplement

North Carolina Superior Court
Unpublished Decisions

North Carolina District Court
Unpublished Decisions

Lawsuits - Civil and/or Criminal

Introduction

There are two types of lawsuits -- civil and criminal; however, a party may be subject to both types of lawsuits for a single act. For example, a person who strikes another without provocation can be charged and tried in criminal court for assault and battery. The victim of the assault can sue the wrongdoer in civil court for committing the tort (civil wrong) of assault and battery.

Civil Suits

Purpose -- to remedy injuries to personal interest.

Goal -- to restore the injured party to his condition before the injury.

Remedy -- monetary compensation for the injuries suffered.

Examples:

An individual might sue for personal injuries received in an automobile accident.

An individual might sue an adjoining landowner for building on his or her property.

An employee might sue an employer for breach of contract.

Criminal Cases

Purpose -- to protect society from antisocial conduct or conduct against public interest.

Goal -- to punish a party for an offense the law recognizes as a crime.

Result -- imposition of a fine, imprisonment, probation, or community service.

Examples:

State brings charges against an individual for possession of illegal drugs.

State brings charges against an individual for breaking and entering a dwelling.

The Judicial System - What's Tried Where?

Federal Judicial System

Jurisdiction B Federal Courts have limited jurisdiction -- they are authorized to hear only certain types of cases.

Federal Question Jurisdiction - Federal Courts have jurisdiction over cases and controversies that arise under the laws, treaties, or Constitution of the United States.

Diversity Jurisdiction - Federal Courts have jurisdiction over cases and controversies that involve citizens of different states.

Amount in Controversy - In cases brought in federal courts, the amount in controversy (amount of damages being sought) must exceed $75,000.

Federal District Court

Trial Court - the federal district court is the trial court of the federal judicial system.

Original Jurisdiction - because the district court is the trial court, it has original jurisdiction as distinguished from appellate jurisdiction.

Number of District Courts - Each state has at least one district court; the more populous states have as many as four. North Carolina has three district courts -- Eastern District, Middle District, Western District. There is a total of 94 district courts in the United States and its territories.

Federal Districts in North Carolina

Examples of Cases and Controversies brought in Federal Court:

Defendant questions the constitutionality of a police officer's warrantless search. Defendant contends the search was a violation of his right to privacy and challenges the constitutionality of the search.

Defendant challenges the constitutionality of a warrantless search of his hotel room pursuant to the Fourth Amendment.

Court of Appeals

Intermediate Appellate Court - Court of Appeals is the second level of the three-tier federal judicial system. These courts serve as an intermediate appellate court between the federal district courts and the United States Supreme Court.

Circuits - There are thirteen circuits which serve specific geographical areas. A federal court of appeals sits in each circuit. North Carolina belongs to the Fourth Circuit Court of Appeals which is located in Richmond, Virginia.

A case is rarely appealed directly from the Federal District Court to the United States Supreme Court.

Supreme Court

Court of Last Resort - The final step in the federal judicial system is the United States Supreme Court. It is the only court created by the Constitution and not by Congress.

Makeup of the Court - the court consists of one chief justice and eight associate justices. All members of the court are appointed by the President; their appointment to the bench is for life.

Writ of Certiorari - Not all cases are reviewed by the Supreme Court. A party that seeks review must petition the Court for a "writ of certiorari." When the Court grants the writ, it indicates it will hear a case. Annually, over 5,000 requests for Writs are made and 150 cases are heard.

Certiorari Denied - The Court's refusal to grant certiorari does not necessarily indicate the Court thinks the issues were correctly decided by the lower court or that justice was done. Basically, the Court simply decides not to hear the case therefore, remaining neutral on the issues.

North Carolina Judicial System

District Court Division

Generally - District Court Division is divided into thirty-four judicial districts and sits in the county seat of each county.

Jurisdiction:

Civil - cases involving amounts in controversy of $10,000 or less. Divorce cases, child support cases, and custody cases are properly the business of the district court.

Criminal - the district court has exclusive original jurisdiction with respect to very minor cases.

Juvenile - district court has jurisdiction over juvenile matters. The cases concern children under the age of sixteen who are delinquent or undisciplined and children under the age of eighteen who are dependent and neglected.

Examples of Cases:

District Court has jurisdiction over persons charged with driving while impaired.

District Court has jurisdiction over juvenile matters; therefore, a juvenile charged with vandalizing school property will be tried in District Court.

Superior Court Division (Court of general trial jurisdiction)

Civil Jurisdiction - Cases involving amounts in controversy of $10,000 or more.

Criminal Jurisdiction - Superior court has exclusive jurisdiction over all felonies (major crimes) and jurisdiction over misdemeanors appealed from a conviction in district court.

Examples of Cases:

Civil - A contract dispute between a contractor and a subcontractor.

Criminal - Individual charged with first -degree murder.

Appellate Division

Court of Appeals - The Court of Appeals is the intermediate appellate court in North Carolina. There is an automatic right of appeal to this court.

Supreme Court - the Supreme Court is the state court of last resort. Death penalty cases and cases in which sentences of life imprisonment are given have a right of automatic appeal to the Supreme Court. Cases which involve a constitutional question and cases in which there is a dissent in the Court of Appeals go to the Supreme Court from the Court of Appeals. All other cases go to the Court by certification -- the Supreme Court determines whether or not it will hear the case.

Decisions of state courts of last resort may be appealed to the United States Supreme Court. Some of the cases may be appealed as a matter of right; however, most of the cases are appealed by certiorari.

What's Reported -- What's Not!

Unpublished Decisions

North Carolina District Court - the judge in a district court case writes an order in which he gives a statement of the facts and a finding of law. The order is issued to the participating parties but is not made available to the public.

North Carolina Superior Court - A court reporter records and transcribes the transcript of the trial. The transcript is made available to the participating parties for purposes of appeal; however, it is not made available to the public.

Published Decisions

Federal Courts

United States District Courts - most of the decisions handed down by the federal district courts are published in the Federal Supplement (F. Supp.). The Federal Supplement is a series of reporters published by Thomson West.

United States Courts of Appeal - most of the decisions handed down by the United States Courts of Appeal are published in the Federal Reporter. The Federal Reporter is a series of reporters published by Thomson West which includes the Federal Reporter (F.), Federal Reporter 2d (F.2d), and Federal Reporter 3d (F.3d).

United States Supreme Court - The decisions of the Supreme Court are published in the United States Reports (U.S.), the official reporter of the Court. In addition, the decisions are published in the Supreme Court Reporter (S. Ct.), a Thomson West publication, and the Lawyers' Edition (L.Ed.) published by Lexis Publishers.

North Carolina Courts

North Carolina Court of Appeals - most of the decisions handed down by the Court of Appeals are published in the North Carolina Court of Appeals Reports (N.C.App.)and the Southeastern Reporter (S.E. and S.E.2d). The North Carolina Court of Appeals Reports are the official state reporter, and the Southeastern Reporter is published by Thomson West.

North Carolina Supreme Court - The decisions of the North Carolina Supreme Court are published in the North Carolina Reports (N.C.), the official reporter of the Court. In addition, the decisions are published in the Southeaster Reporter (S.E. and S.E.2d., a Thomson West Publication.

Checklist for Basic Legal Research

1.   Read the facts carefully, and conduct a preliminary analysis of the problem. As you read the problem, look for the following information:

Jurisdiction - Is this a case which would be filed in state court or federal court?

Keywords - Look for keywords or "buzz words" you will use to locate additional information on this issue.

Time Period - Are you looking for law currently in effect or law in force at some time in the past?

2.   The second step in basic research is to consult secondary sources of law to learn more about the topic.

Secondary sources of law include, but are not limited to, law reviews, encyclopedias, ALR annotations, hornbooks, nutshells, and dictionaries.

Some excellent examples of secondary sources are:

C.J.S. (Corpus Juris Secundum) - Legal Encyclopedia

Am. Jur. 2d (American Jurisprudence) - Legal Encyclopedia

Words and Phrases - Legal Dictionary

Nowak and Rotunda on Constitutional Law - Hornbook

Tribe on Constitutional Law - Hornbook

When you consult the secondary sources, you will want to note the following:

Any references to applicable statutes - the U.S. Code and the codes from the various states are annotated. They cite to both law review articles and cases.

Note citations to relevant cases - secondary sources, especially law reviews are "gold mines" of information. An author of a law review article is meticulous about giving credit to the sources used in research.

Note any reference to Topics and Key Numbers - this information makes it easier to find relevant cases in the digest to the reporters.

3.   If you find an applicable statute, skim the annotations.

Note references to secondary sources you may not have seen in your previous reading.

4.   Read the most promising cases you noted from secondary sources and statutory annotations.

Focus on cases in your jurisdiction. The precedents set by opinions from your jurisdiction are binding on the court. Later you may need to branch out to cases in other jurisdictions.

In your notes, include Topics and Key Numbers of relevant headnotes.

Note the cases cited in the cases you read.

5.   Use a digest to find more cases.

Choose a digest that covers your jurisdiction. Using the narrowest digest possible is most efficient -- you can find Supreme Court Cases in the Federal Digest, but it is faster to use the Supreme Court Digest.

If you already know relevant Topics and Key Numbers, start with those.

Skim the scope note and the analysis (outline) at the start of each topic to get a sense of what is covered.

Skim the case squibs and note relevant cases.

Update - use the pocket part and/or interim pamphlet if there are any.

Use the Descriptive Word Index to find more Topics and Key Numbers. Follow cross references.

To find cases by name, use the Table of Cases or Defendant-Plaintiff Table. If One of the parties to the case is the United States, look for the case under the name of the second party.

6.   Read the most promising cases you found using the digest, take notes, and follow new leads.

[Handout Appendix] Appendix

LegalTrac

Introduction

LegalTrac is an online index to over 800 legal pupblications including all major law reviews, law association journals, specialty publications, and seven legal newspapers. LegalTrac allows students to search, in minutes, eighteen years of issues of more than 800 legal publications for articles written on a specific subject.

Instructions for Accessing LegalTrac

1)   Go the Campbell School of Law web site law.campbell.edu/

2)   Click on Law Library

3)   At the Law Library web page, click on Online Legal Resources.

4)   Under Online Legal Resources, click on Law Reviews.

5)   On the next page, click on InfoTrack Search Bank.

6)   At the next screen, click on the button labeled Proceed.

7)   At this point type in your search.

Sample LegalTrac Search

1.   Enter your search terms.

2.   Enclose phrases in quotation marks.

       Search:
       "Searches and Seizures"

Results:

Subjects containing the words: "searches and seizures"
Searches and Seizures
View 5278 articles or Narrow by subdivision
See also related subjects

Subdivisions of: Searches and Seizures
cases
View 1144 articles
Constitutional Law
view 256 articles

Instructions:

1.   Click on the underlined term to view articles or see related subjects.

2.   To view the 1144 articles under Cases, simply click on the word view.

Results:

Subject: Searches and Seizures Subdivision: constitutional law
Citations 1 to 20 (of 1144)

Select all items on this page

Playing variations on legal themes; federalism, First and Fourth Amendment cases dominate those to be heard this term. (Supreme Court Preview) Marcia Coyle.
The National Law Journal Oct 2, 2000 v23 i6 pA1 col 2 (50 col in)
View abstract and retrieval choices

Disavowing the warrant presumption: Have the exceptions finally swallowed the rule? (Case Note)
Florida Law Review July 2000 v52 i3 p705-713
View extended citation and retrieval choices

Of sniffs, searches, and silent overrulings. (Case Note) Kevin Ward.
OLR Summer 2000 v 19 i3 p625-654
View abstract and retrieval choice

Instructions:

1.   To view either an extended citation or an abstract of an article, click on the underlined option which follows the bibliographic entry.

2.   You may print the entire list of items retrieved or selected bibliographic entries. You may also print an abstract for an article.

3.   To retrieve the abstract for the third entry, simply click on the underlined option.

Results:

Campbell University Law Library
LegalTrac
The National Law Journal, Oct 2, 2000 v23 i6 pA1 col2 (50 col in)

Playing variations on legal themes; federalism, First and Fourth Amendment cases dominate those to be heard this term. (Supreme Court Preview) Marcia Coyle.

Abstract: The themes dominating the cases to be heard by the US Supreme Court in the 2000-2001 term are discussed. These will probably include federalism, freedom of speech, and the Fourth Amendment conditions determining the legality of searches and seizures. Cases on the court's calendar so far are discussed.

Subjects Searches and Seizure -- Litigation
Freedom of Speech --Litigation
Federalism B Litigation
Locations   United States
Gov.Agency   United Stated, Supreme Court B Forecasts
Article A66032069

Using the Digest System

What is a Digest?

The digest has been an essential case-finding tool since 1848. A digest is a multivolume index to the law consisting of major topic headings, thousands of subheadings and short summaries of "points of law." These summaries are commonly referred to as headnotes.

Digests are published for individual states, for groups of states (regional digests), singles courts or court systems, and topical areas of the law.

West Key Number Digest

West key number digests are encyclopedic volumes divided into more than 400 topics. Each topic begins with an outline of its subheadings (the topic analysis), followed by headnotes arranged under the subheadings.

Example of a Topic Analysis:

SEARCHES & SEIZURES

I. IN GENERAL

II. WARRANTS

k101. In general.
k102. Permissible subjects and objects
k103. Authority to issue.
k103.1. _____ In General.
k104. _____ Impartial Magistrate Requirement.
k105. Complaint, application or affidavit.
k105.1 _____ In General.
k106. _____ Persons who may apply for or sign affidavit.
k107. _____ Formal Requirements.
k108. _____ Necessity for writing; oral presentation or supplementation.
k109. Proceedings for issuance.

k110.   Telephone Warrants.

Example of Headnotes under the Subheadings:

SEARCHES & SEIZURES

K13. -----   What constitutes search or seizure.

U.S.Ark. 1909. An order directing a foreign corporation sued for violating the Arkansas anti-trust act, Act Ark, Jan. 23, 1905, Acts, p. 1, to produce as witnesses before a commission certain named officers, agents, directors, and emloyees, and to produce any books, papers, etc., in their possession or under their control relating to the merits of the cause or to any defense does not amount to an unreasonable search and seizure.

Hammond Packing Co., v. State of Ark., 29 S. Ct. 370, 212 U.S. 322, 15 Am. Ann. Cas. 645, 53 L. Ed. 530.

U.S. Cal. 1974. Bank's keeping records of its customers pursuant to the Bank Secrecy Act does not constitute a "seizure," and inasmuch as access to the records is to be controlled by legal process, the record-keeping provision did not give rise to an illegal search and seizure. U.S.C.A. Const. Amend. 4; 12 U.S.C.A. "1730d, 1829b, 1951 - 1959.

California Bankers Ass'n v. Shultz, 94 S. Ct. 1494, 416 U.S. 21, 39 L. Ed. 2d 812.

How to Find Cases Using the Digest

1.   Descriptive Word Index - Look for factual and/or legal terms associated with your issue in the Descriptive Words Index. Each entry in the digest refers you to the West Topic and Key number under which cases involving these factual and/or legal issues have been classified. Jot down the Topic and Key numbers, then look them up in the main digest.

2.   Topic Analysis - Look at the topic outline for relevant categories. Then look under the topic & key number in the digest.

Explanation of Citations

Official Cite
(1) (2) (3) (4) (5) (6)
Roe v. Wade, 410 U.S. 113 (1973).

(1)   Plaintiff/Appellant
(2)   Defendant/Appellee
(3)   Volume number
(4)   United States Reports
(5)   Page number on which the case begins
(6)   Date of Decision

Parallel Cites
(1) (2) (3) (4)
Roe v. Wade, 410 U.S. 113, 93 S. Ct. 705, 35 L. Ed. 2d 147 (1973).

(1)   Name of the Case
(2)   Cite to the U.S. Reports which is the official cite
(3)   Cite to the Supreme Court Reporter which is a West publication
(4)   Cite to the Lawyer's Edition 2d published by Lawyer's Co-op

Cites to Looseleaf Services

(1) (2) (3)
Rosenberger v. Rector and Visitors of the University of Virginia, 115 S. Ct. 2510, 132 L. Ed.2d 700, 63
(4)
USLW 4702 (1995).

(1)   Name of the Case
(2)   Cite to the Supreme Court Reporter
(3)   Cite to Lawyer's Edition 2d.
(4)   Cite to United States Law Week -- a looseleaf publication by the Bureau of National Affairs

Abbreviations:
U.S. - United States Reports
S. Ct. - Supreme Court Reporter
L. Ed. 2d - Lawyer's Edition Second
USLW - United States Law Week

54 F.R.D. 282
(Cite as: 54 F.R.D. 282)

United States District Court, W. D. Pennsylvania.
(Plaintiff)
UNITED STATES ex rel. Gerald MAYO
v.
SATAN AND HIS STAFF.
(Defendant)
Misc. No. 5357.
(Docket Number)
Dec. 3, 1971.
(Date of Decision)

Civil rights action against Satan and his servants who allegedly placed deliberate obstacles in plaintiff's path and caused his downfall, wherein plaintiff prayed for leave to proceed in forma pauperis. The District Court, Weber, J., held that plaintiff would not be granted leave to proceed in forma pauperis who in view of questions of personal jurisdiction over defendant, propriety of class action, and plaintiff's failure to include instructions for directions as to service of process.

Prayer denied.

West Headnotes
(Headnotes written by the Editors)
Federal Civil Procedure k2734
170Ak2734

Plaintiff would not be granted leave to proceed in forma pauperis in civil rights action against Satan and his servants, who allegedly placed deliberate obstacles in plaintiff's path and caused his downfall, in view of questions of personal jurisdiction over defendant, propriety of class action, and plaintiff's failure to include instructions for directions as to service of process. Fed.Rules Civ.Proc. rule 23, 28 U.S.C.A.; 18 U.S.C.A. ' 241; 28 U.S.C.A. ' 1343; 42 U.S.C.A. ' 1983.

*282 Gerald Mayo, pro se.

MEMORANDUM ORDER
(Judge who wrote the opinion)
WEBER, District Judge.
(Opinion of the Court)

Plaintiff, alleging jurisdiction under 18 U.S.C. ' 241, 28 U.S.C. ' 1343, and 42 U.S.C. ' 1983 prays for leave to file a complaint for violation of his civil rights *283 in forma pauperis. He alleges that Satan has on numerous occasions caused plaintiff misery and unwarranted threats, against the will of plaintiff, that Satan has placed deliberate obstacles in his path and has caused plaintiff's downfall.

Plaintiff alleges that by reason of these acts Satan has deprived him of his constitutional rights.

We feel that the application to file and proceed in forma pauperis must be denied. Even if plaintiff's complaint reveals a prima facie recital of the infringement of the civil rights of a citizen of the United States, the Court has serious doubts that the complaint reveals a cause of action upon which relief can be granted by the court. We question whether plaintiff may obtain personal jurisdiction over the defendant in this judicial district. The complaint contains no allegation of residence in this district. While the official reports disclose no case where this defendant has appeared as defendant there is an unofficial account of a trial in New Hampshire where this defendant filed an action of mortgage foreclosure as plaintiff. The defendant in that action was represented by the preeminent advocate of that day, and raised the defense that the plaintiff was a foreign prince with no standing to sue in an American Court. This defense was overcome by overwhelming evidence to the contrary. Whether or not this would raise an estoppel in the present case we are unable to determine at this time.

If such action were to be allowed we would also face the question of whether it may be maintained as a class action. It appears to meet the requirements of Fed.R. of Civ.P. 23 that the class is so numerous that joinder of all members is impracticable, there are questions of law and fact common to the class, and the claims of the representative party is typical of the claims of the class. We cannot now determine if the representative party will fairly protect the interests of the class.

We note that the plaintiff has failed to include with his complaint the required form of instructions for the United States Marshal for directions as to service of process.

For the foregoing reasons we must exercise our discretion to refuse the prayer of plaintiff to proceed in forma pauperis.

(Holding of the Court)

It is ordered that the complaint be given a miscellaneous docket number and leave to proceed in forma pauperis be denied.

Location Guide

Statutory Materials

Federal

Statutes at Large
Wiggins Ground Level

U.S. Code (official edition)
Wiggins Ground Level

U.S. Code Annotated
Wiggins Ground Level

U.S. Code Service
Wiggins Ground Level

U.S. Code Congressional and Administrative News
Wiggins Ground Level

Congressional Record
current year
Wiggins Ground Level
previous years
Carrie Rich Memorial Library

Congressional Information Service
Abstracts & Index (CIS)
Wiggins Ground Level

Statutory Materials

State

Current Codes for All States
Wiggins Basement Level

General Statutes of North Carolina
All Levels, Reserve, & Oak Conference Room

Session Laws of North Carolina
Wiggins Ground Level,
Wiggins Basement, & Kivett Level Two

Case Law Materials

Federal

U.S. Reports (official ed.)
Wiggins Ground Level

Supreme Court Reporter
Wiggins Ground Level

U.S. Reports Lawyer's Edition
Wiggins Ground Level

U.S. Law Week
Reference

Federal Reporter, F.2d, F.3d
Wiggins Basement Level

Federal Supplement, F. Supp. 2d
Wiggins Basement Level

Federal Rules Decisions
Wiggins Basement Level

Federal Digests

Supreme Court
Wiggins Ground Level

All Federal Cases
Wiggins Basement Level

Case Law Materials - State

Regional Reporters

Atlantic Reporter, A.2d
Wiggins Basement Level

North Eastern Reporter, N.E.2d
Wiggins Basement Level

North Western Reporter, N.W.2d
Wiggins Basement Level

Pacific, P.2d
Wiggins Basement Level

South Eastern Reporter, S.E.2d
Wiggins Basement Level

South Western Reporter, S.W.2d
Wiggins Basement Level

Southern, So.2d
Wiggins Basement Level

New York Supplement, N.Y.S.2d
Wiggins Basement Level

California Reporter, Cal. Rptr. 2d
Wiggins Basement Level

North Carolina Reporters

North Carolina Reports
All Levels

Oak Conference Room

North Carolina Court of Appeals Reports
All Levels
Oak Conference Room

West's North Carolina Reporter
Wiggins Basement Level

Digests

Individual States

California Digest
Wiggins Basement Level

Florida Digest
Wiggins Basement Level

Georgia Digest
Wiggins Basement Level

New York Digest
Wiggins Basement Level

South Carolina Digest
Wiggins Basement Level

Virginia & West Virginia Digest
Wiggins Basement Level

Regional

South Eastern Digest, S.E. Digest 2d
Wiggins Basement Level

North Carolina

North Carolina Digest
Kivett Level Two
Wiggins Basement Level
Wiggins Ground Level
Oak Conference Room

Strong's North Carolina Index
Kivett Level Two
Wiggins Basement Level
Wiggins Ground Level
Oak Conference Room

American Digest System

American Digest Decennial Edition
Wiggins Ground Level

Third - Tenth Decennial Digests
Wiggins Ground Level

Administrative Law Materials

Federal

Code of Federal Regulations
Microforms Room

Federal Register
Microforms Room

North Carolina

North Carolina Administrative Code
Kivett Level Two

North Carolina Register
Kivett Level Two

Secondary Sources

American Law Reports

American Law Reports
Wiggins Ground Level

A.L.R. 2d
Wiggins Ground Level

A.L.R. 3d
Wiggins Ground Level

A.L.R. 4th
Wiggins Ground Level

A.L.R. 5th
Wiggins Ground Level

A.L.R. Fed.
Wiggins Ground Level

Encyclopedias

Am. Jur. 2d
Wiggins Ground Level

C.J. S.
Wiggins Ground Level

Dictionaries

Words and Phrases
Wiggins Ground Level

Black's Law Dictionary
Wiggins Ground Level

Forms

Am. Jur. Legal Forms
Kivett Level One

Am. Jur. Pleading and Practice Forms
Kivett Level Two

Current Legal Forms
Kivett Level One

Douglas' Forms
Reserve

West's Legal Forms
Kivett Level One

Law Reviews

Titles Beginning With A -L
Kivett Level 3

Titles Beginning With M - Z
Kivett Level 4

Law Review Indexes

Index to Legal Periodicals
Kivett Level 4

Current Law Index
Kivett Level 4

Current Index to Legal Periodicals
Kivett Level 4

Index to Periodicals Related to the Law
Kivett Level 4

LegalTrac
Kivett Level 3

Restatements

Restatement First
Wiggins Ground Level

Restatement 2d of Agency
Reserve

Restatement 2d of Conflict of Laws
Reserve

Restatement 2d of Contracts
Reserve

Restatement 2d of Judgments
Reserve

Restatement 2d of Property - Landlord and Tenant
Reserve

Restatement 2d of Trusts
Reserve

Restatement 2d of Torts
Reserve

Shepards Citators

Federal
Wiggins Basement Level
(Shelved immediately after the Federal Reporters)

Regional
Wiggins Basement Level
(Shelved immediately after each set of reporters)

Law Reviews
Kivett Level Four

North Carolina
All Levels
(Shelved immediately after the Court of Appeals Reports)

Useful Internet Sites

Law Libraries

Home Pages

Campbell Law Library
http://www.law.campbell.edu/culawlib.htm

Duke Law Library
http://www.law.duke.edu/lib/library.htm

North Carolina Central Law Library
http://www.nccu.edu/law/lawlib

UNC Chapel Hill Law Library
http://library.law.unc.edu/home.shtml

Wake Forest Law Library
http://www.law.wfu.edu/library/

North Carolina Supreme Court Library
www.aoc.state.nc.us/www/public/html/sc _library.htm

Online Library Catalogs

Campbell Law Library
http://library.campbell.edu:8000/

Duke
http://lcweb.loc.gov/z3950/duke.html

North Carolina Central
http://lcweb.loc.gov/z3950/nccu.html

UNC Chapel Hill
http://lcweb.loc.gov/z3950/unc.html

Wake Forest Law Library
http://pcl.wfu.edu/

The Courts

Opinions

North Carolina

North Carolina Supreme Court
www.ncinsider.com//supreme/supco.html

North Carolina Court of Appeals
www.ncinsider.com//appeals/appeals.html

Federal Courts

United States Supreme Court
http://www.supremecourtus.gov/

United States Supreme Court (files at Cornell which are fully searchable)
http://supct.law.cornell.edu/supct/

United States Supreme Court (decisions from 1937 - 1975)
www.fedworld.gov/supcourt/index.htm

All Federal Circuits (Cornell)
www.law.cornell.edu/federal/opinions.html

Fourth Circuit Court of Appeals (Emory)
http://www.law.emory.edu/4circuit/

Federal District Courts
http://fedlaw.gsa.gov/legal32.htm

Middle District of North Carolina
http://www.ncmd.uscourts.gov/

Western District of North Carolina
http://www.ncwd.uscourts.gov/

Constitutions and Codes

North Carolina

Constitution
http://statelibrary.dcr.state.nc.us/nc/stgovt/preconst.htm

General Statutes
www.ncga.state.nc.us

United States

Constitution
http://www.house.gov/Constitution/Constitution.html

Constitution (Amendments)
http://www.house.gov/Constitution/Amend.html

Constitution (Interpretation & Analysis)
www.access.gpo.gov/congress/senate/constitution/

United States Code (Cornell)
http://www4.law.cornell.edu/uscode/

United States Code(GPO Access)
www.access.gpo.gov/congress/cong013.html

United States Code (U.S. House)
http://uscode.house.gov/usc.htm

Public Laws (Current)
http://thomas.loc.gov/bss/d106/d106laws.html

Public Laws (Previous)
http://thomas.loc.gov/home/bdquery.html

Legislative Documents

North Carolina

North Carolina General Assembly (bill status and new legislation)
www.ncga.state.nc.us

United States

Bills
http://thomas.loc.gov/bss/d106query.html

Hearings
www.access.gpo.gov/congress/cong017.html

Committee Reports
http://thomas.loc.gov/cp106/cp106query.html

Congressional Record
http://thomas.loc.gov/j106/j106index1.html

Administrative Law

North Carolina

North Carolina Attorney General Opinions
www.jus.state.nc.us/opinion/agoopn.htm

United States

Code of Federal Regulations (Cornell)
http://www4.law.cornell.edu/cfr/

Code of Federal Regulations (GPO)
http://www.access.gpo.gov/nara/cfr/cfr table search.html

Federal Register
http://www.access.gpo.gov/su_docs/aces/aces140.html

Comprehensive Law Sites

JurisLine
http://www.jurisline.com/homepage.cfm

Meta-Index for U.S. Legal Research
http://gsulaw.gsu.edu/metaindex/

Law Guru
www.lawguru.com/search/lawsearch.html

LIBClient (UNC Chapel Hill)
www.ils.unc.edu/~vreer/libclient/LIBClient.html

Full-Text Search (Washburn)
http://www.washlaw.edu/searchlaw.html

FindLaw (North Carolina)
http://www.findlaw.com/11stategov/nc/

FindLaw
www.findlaw.com

Law Crawler
www.lawcrawler.com

Law Runner/ILRG
http://www.ilrg.com/

Fastsearch
www.fastsearch.com

FirstGov.gov
http://www.firstgov.com/

WashLaw Web (Washburn)
http://www.washlaw.edu/

Legal Research Compass (Villanova)
http://vls.law.vill.edu/compass/

Virtual Library:Law (Indiana University)
http://www.law.indiana.edu/v lib/

Law Engine
http://www.thelawengine.com/

American Law Sources On-Line
http://www.lawsource.com/also/

Courtesy of Olivia Leigh Weeks, Campbell University Norman Adrian Wiggins School of Law